Sucking Up
Yellow Jackets

Raising an undiagnosed
Asperger Syndrome son
obsessed with explosives
and motorcycles
A Memoir

First published by O Books, 2010
O Books is an imprint of John Hunt Publishing Ltd., The Bothy, Deershot Lodge, Park Lane, Ropley,
Hants, SO24 0BE, UK
office1@o-books.net
www.o-books.net

Distribution in:

UK and Europe
Orca Book Services Ltd
tradeorders@orcabookservices.co.uk
directorders@orcabookservices.co.uk
Tel: 01235 465521 Fax: 01235 465555
Int. code (44)

USA and Canada
NBN
custserv@nbnbooks.com
Tel: 1 800 462 6420 Fax: 1 800 338 4550

Australia and New Zealand
Brumby Books
sales@brumbybooks.com.au
Tel: 61 3 9761 5535 Fax: 61 3 9761 7095

Far East (offices in Singapore, Thailand,
Hong Kong, Taiwan)
Pansing Distribution Pte Ltd
kemal@pansing.com
Tel: 65 6319 9939 Fax: 65 6462 5761

South Africa
Stephan Phillips (pty) Ltd
Email: orders@stephanphillips.com
Tel: 27 21 4489839 Telefax: 27 21 4479879

Text copyright Jeanne Denault 2009

Design: Tom Davies

ISBN: 978 1 84694 384 3

A CIP catalogue record for this book is available
from the British Library.

Printed by CPI Antony Rowe, Chippenham,   iltshire

O Books operates a distinctive and ethical publishing philosophy in
all areas of its business, from its global network of authors to
production and worldwide distribution.

Sucking Up Yellow Jackets

Raising an undiagnosed
Asperger Syndrome son
obsessed with explosives
and motorcycles
A Memoir

Jeanne Denault

BOOKS

Winchester, UK
Washington, USA

To my children who encouraged me to be myself and made my life so much richer.

Author's Note

We all remember an event differently. After so many years each person in the story has shaped their own set of memories. When possible, I asked the people who had been present what these were and changed pertinent details. By asking *what* was said rather than *if* someone said what I thought they had, I verified a surprising number of the more vivid statements. Where I couldn't recollect someone's name or was concerned the story might embarrass them, I've used pseudonyms. In the end, this is what I remember.

Acknowledgements

I am grateful to the Rebel Writers of Bucks County who suggested the memoir, gave me endless encouragement and thorough critiques: Marie Lamba, Chris Bauer, Dave Jarrett, John Wirebach. Additional thanks to Damian McNicholl, the Rebel Writer who not only did all of the above but introduced me to Joan Schweighardt who made time to read the manuscript and recommended me to Trevor Greenfield of O-books, who has done a great job of leading me through the publication process. And to Carolyn Burdett, my editor at O-books, who did the excellent final edit. My heartfelt thanks to them all.

And thanks to S. C. Naugler for his computer knowledge and thorough line edit. To Pete who showed me so much of the world I would never have seen without him.

To Vicki, Chris, Jody, Jacqueline, Caitlin, Courtney, Emily, Ainsley and Aidan: my extended family. They brighten my life. And to Nan Ross, who always made me feel whole.

Prologue

"Max started seeing psychologists when he was three and they never told you he had Asperger Syndrome?" Fran looked surprised. "He sounds like a classic Asperger's case study. How could they have missed it?"

"What's Asperger Syndrome?"

"It's a form of autism."

"I thought autistic kids started out normal and lost their ability to talk or interact with people when they were still babies. That sure doesn't describe Max. He's been talking non-stop for the last 40 odd years."

"Yes but does he let *you* talk? Or talk about things that interest you? Can he look at you and tell when you're bored with what he's saying?"

I felt as though a cartoon balloon with a light bulb in it should be popping out of the side of my head as Fran ticked off each trait.

"You've got Max nailed." I agreed. "Those are Asperger's symptoms?"

"Yes. Like other autistic kids, his brain's wired differently from allegedly 'normal' people. You're lucky he's so bright. Silicon Valley's full of people with Asperger's."

"Is there a treatment for it?" I asked.

"Behavior modification, special schooling and support networks for the whole family but only if the child's diagnosed when they're young enough for it to help," she replied. "Most Asperger's kids have obsessions. What's Max's?"

"Explosives and motorcycles."

She raised her eyebrows. "No wonder you still worry about him."

When Fran left, I stared at the stark painting that had always had a prominent place in my living room. In the bottom right of

1

the tall canvas, two small pajama-clad children sat side by side on a barely suggested bench. White paint laid on with a palette knife filled much of the frame but the small figures of two-year-old Max and his three-year-old sister Linda were so arresting they dominated the picture. Painted by their father, Pete, the strokes of color were so assured, the figures had the accuracy of photographs.

Max's blue eyes shone with wide-eyed innocence but his hand was clamped over his mouth. Nothing could get him to take his hand down so Pete painted it just as it was.

I found the painting troubling. It symbolized the craziness of life with Max. He wouldn't tell me why he covered his mouth. Each time I looked at it, I marveled that anyone so inherently sweet could cause so much grief.

Chapter 1

"I'm sick of this shit. We either have to get married or break up," my boyfriend said. It wasn't the sort of proposal you'd see in a romantic movie but it made sense. Pete lived three subway transfers away from me, a mind-numbing trek late at night. He shared a railroad flat with seven men in Brooklyn. And like a train, the only way to get from room to room was to walk through the one before or after it. The apartment was like a people zoo. The only room with a lock was the bathroom in the hall.

I lived in a small room over a dog hospital in mid-Manhattan. I'd been told that if I ever dared bring a man to my room, I'd be booted on the spot. I didn't think my landlords had anything against sex; they were just following the rules of the day. I was a young, single female and grown ups protected *nice* girls against their baser instincts. I had a lot of those where Pete was concerned.

Had it been today, we would have rented an apartment and lived together to see how we meshed when the pheromones stopped dictating our actions, but in the fifties this was virtually impossible. Even movie stars and the wealthy had to get married if they wanted to live together. Serial marriages were okay but living in sin was not condoned.

So we got married. The next line is supposed to be "and lived happily ever after." But fairy tales never tell how the wife and children of Prince Charming fare when the early glow fades.

Before I agreed to marry him, I told Pete I didn't want children for years. I had other things I wanted to do first, such as establishing a career I enjoyed so I could be independent. He said he'd had mumps when he was seventeen and was probably sterile but he didn't care because he wanted to be free to paint.

I don't know if that was what he really thought or if he

3

assumed I couldn't possibly mean what I said. People rarely took me seriously. I was small, my voice was soft and I was inclined to placate rather than argue. Most people looked jolted when I said what I was really thinking so I smiled a lot and kept my thoughts to myself.

For a year, we had what I considered a near-perfect lifestyle. We lived in New York City, in Greenwich Village, in a rent-controlled apartment with a working fireplace, a skylight and French doors opening onto the top of a fire escape. We roamed the city and shared an equal fascination with the weird things we saw. Our friends wanted houses and babies. We wanted to see Europe before the Russians wiped it off the globe.

We rode third-class trains all over Europe for so little money we were able to hop off at will when a town looked worth exploring. We drank beer in England, Holland and Germany, wine everywhere else. I carried a small bag with a liter bottle we refilled with wine in each town, the way the locals did. We lived on bread, cheese, sausages, apples and pears with an occasional hot meal in a cheap restaurant.

In Italy we joined the Communist Party. This had nothing to do with ideology; we both had student cards and had discovered that students who belonged to the Party got excellent seven-course meals with wine included in the "student and worker" restaurants in all the large cities. This was too good to pass up. We decided we would ignore Senator Joseph McCarthy's bizarre reign of fear over Americans with Communist affiliations.

We got visas to travel through Russian territory in Austria. Russian soldiers lined the platforms at every stop to make sure no one but locals disembarked. We were met in Vienna by an official from the American Embassy. We were the only Americans on the train. The official gave us a list of things forbidden in the Russian Sector of the city, waited until we read every word, then made us sign an agreement that we wouldn't contact the American Embassy for any reason before they allowed us to leave

4

the train station. As the embassy official said, "The United States doesn't plan to start World War Three because a couple of dumb kids thought it would be fun to take a picture of a Russian soldier and ended up in prison."

We wandered through the Austrian Alps and down to Trieste where my college room mate and her army officer husband were living with their colicky two-month-old baby. The fourth day we were there, Pete told me he wanted six kids, none more than eighteen months apart and he wanted to start his family right away.

He never told me why he suddenly wanted one child, let alone six. I assumed there was something that had brought about this abrupt turn-around but if so, he kept it to himself. If I hadn't been there I might have thought he had gone all soft and gooey inside at the sight of my roommate's baby, but I saw for myself that he had regarded her with the same lack of interest he might have shown if the baby had been a new pair of shoes. Nice enough but nothing he would wear.

I was outraged but I couldn't even tell my former room mate how I felt. She was enthralled with motherhood. Telling most people I wanted a chance to grow up and test my wings as an individual before I took on the responsibility of children would have had few favorable listeners. This was the fifties when women's lib didn't exist and a woman who didn't want children was considered an aberration.

The billion-dollar spending spree the American government had launched trying to get women back into the home "where they belonged" so returning GIs could take their jobs was waning but it was still pervasive. In the atmosphere of the time, declaring I wanted a life parallel to my husband's was like saying I wanted to be a serial killer.

For the next six weeks, Pete was the only friend available. With few English speakers outside of American Express offices, we were more dependent on each other than we had ever been in

New York City.

Whatever caused his change of heart, Pete was persistent. I tried to reason with him but he couldn't seem to grasp my point of view. I think he was genuinely bewildered. Regardless of what I said, I was a woman; women liked babies. Periods of tenderness alternating with irritation when he barely spoke to me wore me down. I felt as though I were living with my mother again, only I had picked this one so I couldn't escape responsibility.

Unfortunately for me I still found him physically attractive. My pulse still accelerated when I saw him. Errant hormones were lousy at intelligent choices.

With a few witty barbs, he made me felt like a backward child full of dumb ideas about real life if I disagreed with him.

When I continued to insist I didn't want children yet, he finally turned on me, his face twisted with frustration as he said, "What kind of a woman are you?"

This was way below the belt. I had made the mistake of sharing my childhood disappointment at discovering I was a girl. I told him how dismayed I had been when I realized I might end up like my unhappy mother who sighed a lot, rarely finished anything, hung around the house all day in shapeless cotton house dresses and smelled like unwashed hair. I wanted to be like my exciting dad, who went to work wearing suits and starched shirts and smelled of the bay rum and witch hazel aftershave he always used.

The last few weeks we were in Europe were spent in Paris. Pete caught a bad cold. He would have liked me to hang around and wait on him all day but I had other ideas. I was happy to care for him but knew I could do it without sitting on the edge of a sagging bed in a musty smelling room watching him sleep. I bought a thermometer. It was calibrated for Celsius but it had the usual red line that indicated what was considered normal. I showed him how to read it and shake it down then made sure he had food, drink, aspirins and American and English newspapers to read, and then I spent ten blissful days wandering around Paris by myself.

Pete was an exciting traveling companion, full of ideas and endless curiosity. Yet this time on my own was the part of the trip I dreamed about for years. It was the first time during the four and a half months of our wandering when I could move at my own pace and go where I wanted. I enjoyed Pete's company so much I hadn't realized we always ended up going where he wanted and we always left when he said it was time to go.

For years after that trip, I dreamed of walking along the Seine looking across the river at the sun-lit houses on the Ile de la Cité.

In mid-November the late afternoon light had the crystalline transparency of lemon ice. I always wakened from these dreams with a profound sense of loss. And guilt, because part of the hold this brief respite had on my mind was the realization it was the last time I could have made different choices and fervently wished I had.

Sometimes I ate breakfast or lunch with Pete while he was sick but I always ate dinner alone. The concept of take-out food brought a stunned glaze to restaurant owners' eyes. I brought Pete bread, cheese, fruit and wine but after a day of roaming, I wanted a hot sit-down meal. Knowing I was content to eat in a restaurant without him drove Pete crazy. I couldn't figure out why. He insisted there had to be something wrong with me. No normal woman would be comfortable being alone in such a public place. He used the 'normal' word a lot, generally to describe what I wasn't.

When he started to feel better, he bathed, shaved, resumed his "let's make a baby" campaign and turned on his considerable charm. After ten days of watching him do nothing but feel sorry for himself, cough bad breath at me and blow his nose, he was irresistible. Paris was a romantic place. Our room was on the top floor, with windows looking out over moonlit rooftops. I wavered. Once was enough. I was pregnant before I had time to reconsider.

Chapter 2

Two hours after we arrived in New York, we got an urgent phone call from Melrose, Massachusetts. Pete's mother had been diagnosed with kidney cancer and was scheduled to have the diseased kidney removed the following day. We grabbed our still-packed bags and took the next train to Boston.

The cancer turned out to be a particularly virulent form. She was given six months or less to live. (She lived cancer-free for forty more years but that's another story.) I assumed we would be in Melrose just long enough to arrange for her care and would visit her on weekends. We had jobs waiting for us and an apartment we had been paying rent on for the last five months.

Pete was a wreck. His relationship with his widowed mother, Ada, was difficult even when she was healthy. Knowing she was going to die what would probably be a long, agonizing death, triggered a touching need to finally do something to please her. But what? As far as she was concerned he had never done anything right.

She was a strange woman. I sometimes wondered if she had some sort of disconnect between her mouth and her mind. Shortly after she told me her older son, Max, had died in a plane crash, she said, "Why did *he* have to be the one who died?"

Since Pete was the only other person in the family, this was such an appallingly cruel comment I should have beaten a rapid retreat from him and his strange mother, but I just felt unbearably sorry for him. He had heard his mother say this many times before. As I watched, his face assumed the wooden expression I had seen before when he wanted to ignore what I was saying. For the first time I realized this ability to shut out another person was something he had learned as a way to survive his mother.

Our situation with Ada was complicated by the fact that the doctor insisted we not tell her or anyone else she was fatally ill.

Ridiculous as this might sound today when comple[ ]
is mandated, secrecy was the accepted practice with
fifties.

Pete decided we should be there when his mother came nome
from the hospital. I was getting anxious. His marrying me was
currently near the top of Pete's major failures in his mother's
eyes. I was the last person she would want taking care of her. It
would have been easy and relatively inexpensive to hire a live-in
companion for the period of time when she was still mobile and
a nurse when she finally needed one as she went downhill, but
Pete insisted his mother would be more comfortable having
family stay with her until she could manage on her own. Any
suggestion that we should direct her care but get on with our
own lives earned his insistence that 'normal' families put aside
their own needs and took care of each other.

I felt used when it became clear he expected me to be the
primary care-giver not just of my mother-in-law but of the
house, yard, laundry and even the garbage. I didn't have the self-
confidence to fight back. I knew I could do everything Pete
expected of me and do it well. I just didn't want to. This attitude
was crossing the line into selfishness: a deadly sin second only to
murder in my needy, self-centered mother's opinion. Twenty
years of having it drummed into me that I was a bad person if I
was selfish enough to put my own needs ahead of my mother's
had trained me well.

Here was this poor woman with a death sentence over her
head. How could I be so cavalier about her care? I stifled my
feelings and tried harder. Just below the surface, a part of me
simmered. I knew I had become my own worst enemy but I
didn't know what to do, short of walking out, and I wasn't ready
for that.

I bolstered my spirits by reassuring myself that this would
just be a brief side step. I made sure the New York apartment
rent was paid and had the mail forwarded so I could pay the

phone and Con Ed bills. I figured I would get back to my real life as soon as Pete's mother died.

We had stashed money in the bank in case our jobs fell through before we'd started on our European trip. Carrying the expenses of Ada's house and the New York apartment was depleting this money rapidly so we went into Boston and answered a small art studio's ad for artists. We were both hired. These jobs established a recurring pattern that worked but played havoc with my ego. Pete became the designated illustrator. This made sense. He was a gifted and well trained illustrator. He said I was the better designer but he ended up doing that too. I became the hand letterer, type expert and paste-up person because "I was so much better at it than he was."

A month later I visited the family doctor who confirmed I was pregnant.

That was when Pete told me he didn't think New York City was a good place to raise children. Even if we both worked, we couldn't afford a larger apartment and childcare.

I understood how Alice felt when she ended up in Wonderland. Everything was right and wrong at the same time. I knew Pete had a point. Neither of us had been working long enough to make much more than minimum wage but we were both good at what we did and we always had work. Why couldn't we manage? We wouldn't have to move. Our apartment was large enough to section off a space for a crib and a changing table.

Then Pete told me he didn't want to live in New York City. He didn't plan to go back there regardless of what happened with his mother.

I couldn't have been more disoriented if I had awakened in the middle of the Sahara Desert surrounded by camel-riding Arabs who didn't speak English. The existence I had helped create in New York City represented everything I had ever wanted from life.

Pregnancy made me feel painfully vulnerable. My mental

scenario of the kind of life I would have in New York with a baby in tow and no husband gave me chills. Sometimes a vivid imagination is a curse. It was hard to decide if the major problem was lack of courage, innate pragmatism, or too much pride to openly acknowledge I had made a series of really dumb decisions. Probably all of the above.

I went into a profound depression when we gave up our New York apartment. I still remember how my spirits plunged deeper and deeper with each box I carried down the five flights of stairs. It was one of those turning points when you knew you were on a downhill slide and had to accept the fact that you were too chicken to dig in your heels and bring yourself to a screeching halt.

As we drove back to Melrose dragging our meager possessions behind us in a small borrowed trailer, I felt as though the world had been blanketed by a dark, bitterly cold fog. Pete didn't notice. It's hard to fault him for this. We were well matched. I was good at covering my feelings. He was equally good at not noticing what he didn't want to see.

Strong emotions upset him. He never talked about his feelings. I was never sure he even acknowledged them to himself. With no verifiable data from him, I had to do a lot of guessing and piecing together reasons for everything he did or didn't do. And after that lengthy exercise, I had to spend an equal amount of effort concocting what I considered to be reasonable excuses for his actions so that I could live with them without getting frazzled.

Since our brains worked differently, I often ascribed motives to him that were probably a long way from what he was really thinking. I was working from a base of Jane Austen and the Brontes, where spirited women conquered cold and distant men like Darcy and Rochester. It took me a long time to understand that emotionally remote men were not turned into considerate, tender husbands by any women other than the hopeful authors.

I was sorry my mother had not been interested in history instead of nineteenth century novels. I might have had fewer illusions about the inherent capacity of love to change stone-faced characters if my young mind had been exposed to real-life tales of men like Caligula instead of Mr. Darcy.

Pete read magazines and newspapers. He rarely read novels. His understanding of male/female relationships was formed by watching his parents wage a never-ending war for control of their small household. Nothing was ever resolved. When the skirmishes grew too vicious, his parents stopped speaking to each other, once for a full year. Far from giving Pete a respite, during these breaks he was forced to be the conduit as his feuding parents each did their best to verbally annihilate the other. Pete had learned to slip out of the house without telling either parent where he would be in order to stay sane. Yet he insisted they were normal. He may have believed it.

Pete insisted my family was a clump of crazies so I couldn't possibly know how 'normal' families functioned. I couldn't refute this. My siblings were great but my mother was more or less acceptable at times and certifiably nutty at others. The trick was figuring out which mother was waiting behind the closed door. She disowned people for periods of time—sometimes for years. No money or real property was involved. She just pretended the shunned person didn't exist. For example; she hadn't wanted me to marry. This wasn't because she thought Pete would or wouldn't make a good husband. As far as I could see, she liked him. It was just one of her freaked-out periods. She warned my father she would leave him if he went to my wedding. He came anyway. She went to Florida and moved in with her mother. She went back to my father a few months later but she would have nothing to do with me for years. By the time she did grudgingly acknowledge me, I had two children. She was never a doting grandmother. Being the shunned one was upsetting but I didn't understand how pathologically weird it was until I had children

12

of my own. Anything seemed normal if it happened often enough.

My dad was high functioning at work but volatile at home. Deep down, I knew his irritation was impersonal. He even kicked the dog out of the way once and he talked baby talk to her so he obviously loved her.

I only deduced that Pete's family members were as wacky as mine through observation. He never admitted it but once the initial ardor of our affair faded and I allowed myself to look at the two family members I knew with a proximity-jaded eye, it baffled me that I had ever believed anything about Pete's family was as he had said. It's hard to believe I didn't acknowledge this earlier. Shortly after I met Pete, I asked if he had siblings. He said, "No" without hesitation. The first time I met his mother, she talked about someone named Maxwell. I finally asked who this person was. The poor woman burst into tears. She never believed me when I said Pete hadn't told me he had an older brother who had died during the war. He later insisted he had given me an honest answer. Raised in the Congregational Church, he didn't understand sins of omission.

Chapter 3

We stuck to the promise we gave the doctor to not tell Ada she was dying from cancer, so she assumed we were freeloaders. She equated artists with self-indulgent wastrels who sponged off their families and she continually berated Pete for not getting a 'real' job. The fact that we paid all the bills and bought most of the food didn't seem to make any difference. This and the fact that Pete had gotten into the habit of slipping out of the house without telling me where he was going as soon as Ada and I started washing dishes turned life with Pete's mother into a bad sit-com.

Three months before our first child was born, we realized Ada wasn't planning to die in the near future so we moved to a large apartment on the first block of Commonwealth Avenue in downtown Boston. The Public Gardens with their swan boats and serpentine, tree-shaded walks were half a block away. The main room in our apartment had been the formal dining room in one of the very large four-story townhouses lining both sides of the wide avenue. It was an impressive space, with a twelve-foot ceiling and a large fireplace with an ornate marble mantel. Three floor-to-ceiling windows formed a bay overlooking a courtyard. Our bedrooms were in the old servant's quarters.

Giving my first child a name she had to drag around for the rest of her life seemed egocentric, as though I thought someone had elected me God because I'd produced a baby. Friends were visiting the night before I left the hospital with my still un-named daughter. The charge nurse came into my room and told me I had better give my baby a name before she sent in the paperwork or the child's first and second names would legally be Infant Female until we petitioned the court to change them. One of the friends reeled off a string of names she planned to give her kids. Pete and I both liked Linda, the least flowery name the friend mentioned.

14

We didn't bother with a second name.

Linda was an anxious, colicky baby who waked screaming if a bird chirped near her window. When I saw pictures of me taken during this period, I looked starry-eyed. I was actually sleepwalking most of the time.

To my amazement, I discovered I had inherited my grand-mother's strong maternal instinct. I realized I loved this cranky little girl. She was opinionated and loved to eat—my kind of girl. By the time she was four months old, she could look sideways through her eyelashes at me in a way that said "don't try to kid me, lady" as clearly as if she had said it. I spent a ridiculous amount of time carrying her in the crook of one arm and talking to her. She made me laugh.

One very cold winter day when Linda was six-months old, Pete walked into the apartment and said that I should stop nursing her. It was time to start the second child. I had no idea what triggered this. It was too soon. Linda was a great kid but she still hadn't figured out the sleeping-at-night part.

By then I had grasped the fact that I would never dissuade Pete from doing exactly what he wanted to do. I was too tired to fight with him. He had a game plan and he had cast me as the person who supported his dreams no matter what this cost me.

Unfortunately, this was the classic male/female ideal of the time so he had a lot of support. Our friends at the time were people he had known all of his life. The men and most of their wives were at least five years older than I was and had between two and five children. None of the women worked or had any desire to work outside of the home. I was good at faking cheer-fulness but I felt as though I went through my days with an elephant sitting on my chest.

My mother had been fond of saying her family members were so proud and well-mannered they could serve tea to a stranger in the front room with aplomb even if they knew a relative was committing a murder in the back of the house. They were four generations removed from Germany but the need to keep up appearances was part of their DNA.

I sometimes wondered if the rest of my life would have been easier and more honest if I had been able to have a noisy, obvious nervous breakdown. Maybe not.

I would have had to do something really out of character, like wheel Linda down the middle of Commonwealth Avenue with both of us stark naked. Even then, if Pete were the first one to see me, he would probably have draped his coat over my shoulders and asked me if I had baked the lemon meringue pie he'd told me he wanted for dinner.

Chapter 4

I anticipated going through the problem with names when the second child was born. When Pete was told he had a son, he said, "He will be named Maxwell." His voice was flat and ponderous like those fake God voices issuing from roiling clouds in B movies. He's given to sarcastic statements. I was about to laugh but the look on his face stopped me. He was serious.

The name was okay with me but I was surprised. My mother-in-law talked about *her* Maxwell non-stop. She said he was a saint. I was looking at her face when Pete told her *our* son would be called Maxwell. She flinched and looked jolted. Not happy. More like, "How dare you?" When I mentioned that his mother didn't seem pleased at the idea of a second Maxwell, Pete shrugged and said, "Nothing I do pleases her."

He still insisted we name our son Maxwell but called him Ralph. This infuriated his mother. I sometimes wondered if that was the point of the whole naming fiasco. I felt sad that an innocent little boy was secondary to the ongoing mother-son love-hate fest. Pete's mother was programmed to consider the baby a usurper from the start. I probably added to her grief when I started calling him Max.

My mother-in-law was a disaster as a parent and in-law but a very good businesswoman. She ran a successful hooked rug-making enterprise out of her house. Her most important source of income came from packets of wool dyed in each of the myriad colors used for the rugs. She dyed fine wool flannel into values ranging from almost white to the full color of the dye, tore the fabric into precise four-by-eight inch pieces and stapled these together with a hand-written label. In her copper-plate script, the exotic color names looked elegant and expensive.

They were. She had a gift for marketing.

The packets were displayed in a custom-made floor to ceiling, window to window case in the back bedroom she used as her classroom. The display shelves looked like a hotel mail rack on steroids. This dyed wool required numerous bolts of fine wool flannel and frequent trips to the woolen mill north of Concord where Pete and I had moved when Max was a month old. These forays were taken some time between five and six in the morning so she could be at the mill when it opened and back home in time for her students.

She frequently stopped at our house in those very early morning hours, barged into the kitchen and then into Pete's and my bedroom without knocking. This unhinged me. I told her I would appreciate it if she knocked. She didn't even acknowledge I had said anything. I complained to Pete. "Can't you tell her to knock?"

He looked defeated. "What makes you think she'll pay any attention to what I say?"

"What will we do if we're having sex when she barges in? Can't we at least lock the bedroom door?"

The reference to sex elicited a "so what" shrug but the comment about locking a door grabbed his attention. His voice flat and cold, he looked at me through narrowed eyes as he said, "I better never find one of my doors locked."

This was an old issue but it seemed so ridiculous, I kept testing his parameters. I wasn't sure what he would do if he were confronted by a locked door but his tone of voice and cranky expression convinced me I probably would be better off if I didn't have to find out.

He let me lock our apartment door when we lived in New York City and occasionally in downtown Boston but never in Melrose or Concord. This kept me on edge. I was raised by a fanatical door-locker. My father not only locked every door, he went back and made sure they were still locked by checking and rechecking every window twice. It was a large house so this took a while. I assumed this obsessive concern was needed to set his mind at ease but it had the opposite effect on me. I was sure he was the most formidable man in the world. If he were so afraid of whatever lurked out there, it must be pretty bad. With my child's imagination I decided bears, lions and witches must live in the dark woods my bedroom windows faced. Afraid to go to sleep and jerking awake at any unusual night sound, I practiced breathing so I didn't move the covers and arranged my pillows so anyone really bad wouldn't realize there was a live body in my bed.

Explaining to Pete why I preferred locked doors at night didn't get me anywhere. He just laughed at my father's compulsive nature. I don't think he realized he was just as obsessive. Asking him why he hated locked doors just made him grit his teeth and glare at me with the irritated expression he usually saved for his mother's yapping Pomeranian when it had the temerity to lunge at him and try to nip his leg. I couldn't decide if he had no introspection at all or didn't want to acknowledge something dark inside his mind. I suspected it was a little of both.

Each time something came out of left field like his aversion to locks, I was amazed at how little I understood what went on in Pete's mind. Even with the locks, I was never able to figure out if he hated the idea of being locked in or locked out. How could I have dated him for two years, theoretically talked intelligently with him and been married to him for four years and still be so startled at what he expected? I still thought he was the most physically attractive and certainly the wittiest person I had ever known, but more and more frequently wished I had never met him.

Pete's mother continued to be one of those vexing problems common with people who were thrown together but never meshed. Although I admired her in many ways I didn't like her from the first time we met and the dislike was mutual. To her, I was the woman who "stole her son," turned a religious boy into an agnostic, didn't discipline her only grandchildren, or bathe them, or dress them in starched and ironed clothes, or keep the house white-glove spotless. And I read too much.

To me, my mother-in-law was the rude, overbearing woman who could turn anything she was given into a negative. Giving her a gift was an exercise in frustration. It was either wrong and she took it back then insisted we had spent too much for shoddy goods or when I resorted to potted plants she couldn't take back, she denied she got them even when they were blooming on a glass shelf for anyone to see.

We were expected to appear at her home or host large gatherings in our own house at every holiday. She waited until there was a crowd gathered around then sniped at us. Pete never replied to her attacks on him directly. He waited until one of her friends inevitably asked him where he worked now. Looking innocent, he'd say, "I'm unemployed."

His mother's face predictably reddened with shame then seemed to swell with fury. No one in her rigid middle-class world had ever heard the term "freelance." Real men had nine-to-five jobs they held for life. Anyone else was lower-class and probably sweaty.

Chapter 5

A thud sounding like a cat jumping off a high place came from Linda and Max's bedroom. Jolted from deep sleep, I leaped out of bed and ran, cracking my right elbow as I skidded around the corner through the children's open door. We didn't have a cat.

Within seconds I was crouched over my keening seven-month-old son, my sleep-dulled brain trying to process the sight in front of me. Max was on the floor next to his crib. I stifled my instinct to pick him up. His spine could have been broken. I felt his small body. No sickening divots in his downy head. His joints moved only where they should. Doing my best to keep his spine straight, I slid my shaking hands under him, lifted his small body and tucked him against my shoulder. My heart lurched with relief when he clung to me.

Something was wrong. Seven-month-old babies didn't fall out of cribs. The sides were too high. I must not have checked the side rail latch last night. My stomach felt as though it was trying to squeeze up to the back of my throat. Appalled at my carelessness, I didn't even glance at the bed.

Poor innocent baby; his misplaced faith in my ability to keep him safe started me sniveling. I held him close, rocked side to side, closed my eyes and crooned. "I'm so sorry. I won't ever leave the side unlatched again." Max started shivering. It was early May, still cold in Massachusetts and he was a small, skinny baby. I reached for a blanket in his crib and banged into a wooden slat. I really looked at the crib for the first time. The side was up. I grabbed the bar and shook it. It was locked.

Who did this? He couldn't climb out of a crib without help. With Max clutched against my chest, I tore through all three floors of the small house. There was no one except his still sleeping twenty-two-month-old sister in the crib on the other side of their small bedroom and his snoring father. I didn't wake

21

Pete. After four years of marriage, I knew not to wake him unless the house was on fire.

I went into the living room and sat in the rocker handed down through Pete's family for generations. Someone should have used it for kindling long ago. The runners were too short and the back so tall any person with short legs who made the mistake of sitting back and rocking ended up flat on their back with their feet up in the air. I'm short but careful. And it was the only chair in the living room.

I leaned forward, rocked in a slow tick-tock and tried to accept the fact that my small baby had climbed out of his crib without help. I found it easier to think some infant-hating monster was lurking off-stage. A deranged person wanting to harm a baby was a threat I could solve by picking up the phone and asking for help. There was no help with small children who ignored normal growth stages.

I had been on edge ever since his pediatrician came into my room three hours after Max was born, plunked himself into the visitor's chair, shook his head and said, "This baby's going to give you trouble. He's been wide awake ever since he was born and looking around as though he's trying to decide how to redesign the world."

I was a creative worrier but never expected he would start climbing out of his bed before he could stand up. I should have. Max was strong, he hated to be confined and already showed ruthless tenacity as strong as his father's when he wanted something.

He relaxed slowly. Still a mass of twanging nerves, I took rare comfort from his clinging body. He didn't usually let me hold him for long unless he wanted something beyond his reach. Each time he put his arms in the air to be picked up, I felt a rush of tenderness. Maybe this time he just wanted to be hugged. Instant disappointment followed when he reared away from me and pointed at what he wanted. It was never me. He would have been

22

happier with a robot he could control. Or his father. On the rare occasions when Pete hugged him, Max didn't so much hug back as tolerate the hug and not immediately struggle to be put down. I was grateful for this. I should have been jealous but I wasn't. Any sign of affection or even tolerance Pete showed for his small son warmed my heart.

Linda was so much more rewarding as an infant. I was sure I represented food, transportation and comfort to her in equal measure but she seemed to grasp my reflexive need for pay-back. If I hugged her, she hugged back. She loved to have me snuggle her against my neck and croon silly songs and rhymes to her. She asked to be picked up in order to reach something on occasion, usually food, but she was much less needy and far more appreciative. If she did want me to be a convenient elevator, she would smile at me or give me a small hug of thanks.

This never seemed to occur to Max. I couldn't decide if this was because he was smart enough to figure out he didn't have to beguile me to get food, transportation and dry diapers or if some part of his personality had been left out. He didn't seem to mind if I hugged him as long as I put him right down so he could get on with something more important like dismantling one of his toys.

No light showed from my friend Mary's house across the street at this late hour. Steady drizzle darkened the moonless sky visible through the large picture window with its two flanking double-hung windows, an architectural feature that was an inevitable part of the front façades of houses built in the nineteen-fifties. The owl who lived in one of the enormous creek willows behind the house hooted three times. The repeated sound was a mixture of threat and melancholy. It matched my mood.

The next day I sat in Mary's kitchen watching her knead bread. I told her Max had climbed out of bed. Eyes half-closed against the curling thread of smoke from the cigarette clamped in the corner of her mouth, she considered this. Pausing in her kneading, she plucked the cigarette out of her mouth and rested it on the ashtray on the far end of the counter. "I'm not surprised. Look at him over there. God knows how many objects are in that basket. Fifteen? Twenty? Whatever. Each time he comes over, he takes out each one, gives the ones he had seen before a cursory glance then finds the new ones and checks them over as though he has to describe them for an inventory list. Once he's satisfied that he knows them inside and out, they're relegated to the known list and they get just a cursory glance the next time you bring him over."

I slumped against the counter. "Maybe he has a career in inventory control."

Mary snorted with laughter, picked up her cigarette, inhaled deeply then ground it out in the ashtray. Smoke oozed out of her mouth as she spoke. "I don't even know how to place him on a normal infant behavior chart. Having the ability to remember large numbers of unrelated objects and immediately identify new ones aren't milestones in any of my books."

For the next two weeks Max rattled the bars of his crib with obvious frustration but didn't climb out. I gradually relaxed and stopped leaping out of bed each time a squirrel jumped on the roof. I took him to the pediatrician. Maybe he would tell me the whole incident was a fluke. I should have known better. The doctor had a reputation for brutal honesty.

He shook his head and said, "I've only run across a few boys like your son. He's physically hyperactive and will be obsessive about some things but won't fit the classic obsessive/ compulsive diagnosis. If it's any consolation, boys like Max are usually a great deal brighter than average. But they can be wearing to live with. They seem to operate by a different set of rules. I wish I knew why, but I don't. The one thing I do know is he won't stop trying to get out of his crib if that's what he really wants to do." The frank pity in his eyes was like a hard punch under my rib cage. Sometimes honesty sucks.

Instinctively protective, I clutched a resisting Max against my chest. Acknowledging my gesture, the doctor looked sad. "You can't save him from himself. All you can do is pad the floor next to the crib, put a gate across the doorway and take everything but the cribs out of the room. Don't even leave a dresser there. He can use that to climb on. That should work for a while."

Driving home I had a hard time concentrating on the erratic traffic on Route 128. Linda and Max were blessedly quiet for the moment. I was grateful. I was too tired to deal with all this garbage that was being dumped on me. I wanted to pound the wheel and yell obscenities but I was afraid I wouldn't be able to stop if I gave way to my frustration. I had a temper and a fear of losing control and doing something I would regret. Like many of my characteristics, this sense that I was inherently faulty had been fostered by my mother. She could turn as cold and damaging as dry ice but she rarely lost her temper.

A large car cut across my lane. The man driving aggressively didn't even glance at me. I braked hard and fought the impulse to crash into his car and scream, "Take that you asshole."

I knew I was pushing my luck. I was pretty good at squelching what I was really feeling if it was socially unacceptable by my standards but I was afraid Route 128 would push me beyond my limits so I took the Lexington exit instead of Route 2 even though doing this would add another twenty minutes to the ride.

Concord, Massachusetts was a beautiful old town. Most of the stores, houses and the sprawling Concord Academy were painted white with black shutters. Our house was new: what was locally called a Cape Cod. I was never sure why. I could picture builders in other parts of the country using that name but the Cape was less than an hour's drive from Concord and the structure didn't look like any of the old houses I had seen there. It was small, solid, well-built and looked like a tidy box painted gray. Except for the color, it was exactly like the eleven other houses in the first small housing development in Concord. Not that the locals admitted we were part of the town. They referred to us as those tacky new houses out in the old potato field.

The numbing fatigue that had become a constant in my world still fogged my thinking but the peaceful old road with its ancient homes and weathered barns at the end of dusty lanes had a calming effect. I managed to stay reasonable when Linda screamed as I drove right past the ice cream store without stopping. By the time we finally got to the center of Concord, Max was howling along with her. I liked to think this was a show of empathy but suspected it was probably his discomfort at the decibel level his sister reached. Max was sensitive to loud noise and Linda had a piercing shriek that made my eardrums ache.

Our car wasn't air conditioned and it was a warm day so the front windows were open. We sailed around the staid town square broadcasting a racket that must have sounded like a caged pack of out-of-control hyenas. Heads turned. No one smiled. I pretended I was invisible. I was good at that. I'd had a lot of practice.

Chapter 6

The night after our visit to the pediatrician, Max climbed out of his bed again. I assumed the padding encouraged him to think I agreed with his escape attempt and wanted to save him the pain of landing on the unforgiving oak floor. When I heard the thump, I struggled out of bed stupefied with fatigue. The accordion gate pinched his feet and slowed him down. This gave me an extra few seconds to gather my wits together. It must have been daunting for this tiny boy to make the decision to drop to the floor. His heart was still beating a staccato tempo when I lifted him off the gate and put him back in his crib.

A part of me was touched by the hopelessness he must have felt but a larger part had to fight down the desperate need to shriek with frustration. His enormous blue eyes looked sad but he didn't protest. This made me feel even worse.

I wished I didn't worry so much about the way other people felt. This empathy got in my way when I had to discipline Linda or Max. I told him I was sorry and asked him to please stay in his crib until it was time to get up. I explained about morning and what daylight looked like. I tried to stay calm but I could hear the rising tension and frustration in my voice. I was sure Max heard it too. He watched me and looked remote as I babbled on. I was certain he understood what I said but I had the uncomfortable feeling he was humoring me. He was just waiting until I left so he could take a brief nap and make another try for freedom. Which he did, night after night.

I hadn't gone through all the normal stages of sleep since Max was born. Some indomitable maternal instinct kicked in just before I was about to sink into the hard to rouse but mind and spirit renewing deep sleep that allowed the sleeper to awake refreshed and ready to face a new day. I never wanted to face the new day. I was only twenty-four years old. I should have been full of energy but I felt half-dead.

Linda had just turned two. She should have been throwing her weight around and having tantrums but she rarely did. I got the impression she was as overwhelmed by Max's attention-demanding, anti-social behavior as I was and decided much too young to be the good kid. When I tried to give her the time I knew she needed, Max took advantage of my brief lack of vigilance and did something that required my instant attention.

The two children had to share a room. Cape Cod houses had two bedrooms and a bath on the first floor with stairs and space for two more rooms and a second bath on the top floor. The upper story was still unfinished except for roughed-in wiring and plumbing. The floor was raw plywood. We insulated the entire space and put in radiators so we could use it as an art studio but we hadn't done any further finishing.

Linda hated being closed in. She had a rare tantrum when I told her I would have to close her bedroom door from now on. She shrieked, "No — no — no. *My* room. Want *my* door open." She pitched toys at the wall. I felt like joining her. Smashing a few objects with satisfying crunches would have felt good.

Doctor Spock was the reigning guru of child rearing at that time; I wasn't sure what he would have suggested under the circumstances. I worked hard at behaving the way I thought a reasonable adult should and tried to explain. I let her pitch toys until she was calm then crouched and stood her in front of me so our faces were level. "I'm sorry, Linda. I have no choice. I can't put Max up on the second floor even if I put a gate at the top of the stairs. All the wiring is still exposed. I can't put you up there. The shiny insulation scares you even in the daytime. With Max climbing out of his crib all night long, I'll end up batty from fatigue if I don't close the door."

She yanked her shoulders out of my hands, glared at me and turned to Max with a venomous expression. If she were in a cartoon, arrows would have been shooting out of her eyes and stabbing him in the heart.

I felt guilty but not guilty enough to leave the door open. Linda could have climbed out of her crib if she had wanted to; she could open doors easily. I didn't know why she stayed in her bed and sulked instead. I worried that Max was making her feel as impotent as I felt dealing with a child who was catered to because he ignored all the rules. He continued to climb out of his crib but he was still too short to reach the door knob so he spent a lot of nights curled up on the floor. I was tempted to stop giving him vitamins.

Chapter 7

I daydreamed to get through the exhausting boredom of my days. This made it possible to iron a lot of shirts. In my daydreams I was often a widow. This idea sometimes brought me to tears but continued to slide into my mind with the persistence of a New York City cockroach. As a widow, I was saddened by my loss but not responsible for fate. I hadn't given up on my commitment to love, honor and obey. Chance had taken away the object of my undying love. I was just superstitious enough to think I might be pushing my luck so I was careful to keep the life insurance payments up to date.

Magical Thinking persists longer than we would like to acknowledge.

Divorce would have been a more logical daydream but, although I had witnessed many unhappy marriages, my own parents' being a prime example, I had never personally known anyone who was divorced. I wasn't sure what the emotional consequences of such a split would be to me but was certain it would be devastating to my children. They weren't old enough to understand the difference between a chosen relationship and a genetic one. To a small child, rejection was an absolute and would become a terrifying possibility for them. No matter how difficult my marriage was, my children were going to be part of a strong, cohesive family whatever the cost to me. This was more important than my marriage vows.

In the fifties, magazines portrayed all women as happy house-wives who wanted nothing more than to try the new salad advertised in full-page, four-color magazine ads on smooth chrome-coat stock. The ads assumed all husbands came home with nothing on their minds but the excellent meal waiting for them. Any woman who didn't think this was a rich, fulfilling life was told her thought processes were at fault.

One of the more popular women's magazines had a feature asking, "Can this marriage be saved?" Each month I bought the magazine and flipped straight to the article, hoping the expert would finally say, "No way." But no matter how bizarre the couple's problems were, the end result was usually, "Yes, if..." And the "if" always seemed to be something the wife could do.

When I see reprints of ads from that era, they look so ridiculous; it's hard to imagine anyone paying attention to them. But we did, because there was nothing else. It was assumed women would spend their days taking care of their husbands, their children and their houses, in that order. The only recreation for women in most suburbs was the coffee klatch. A second car was rare. Unless the husband was in a car pool so he didn't need the car every day, the only people available for any sort of daytime get-together were neighbors.

I was lucky to be in Concord. I had never pictured living in a country town. We ended up there almost by chance. Driving home from a visit to a friend's house in Littleton, we decided to take a side trip through Lexington and saw a builder's sign shortly after we turned off Route 2. We drove around the small complex and liked what we saw. The following week we went back and looked at the house that was nearly ready for sale. It's almost embarrassing but I fell in love with the possibility of having my own washer and dryer. I had been hand-washing all of Linda's clothes and hanging them on one of those wheeled clotheslines that stretched between one of the tall windows in our living room and a second wheel attached to one of our bedroom window frames. Pete's and my clothes were dragged to a dirty, crowded laundry out near Boston University or washed and hung to dry at my mother-in-law's house. This had been tiring but possible with one child. I wasn't looking forward to doing it with two babies. So we bought the house. It had a good train into Boston and wonderful neighbors.

Linda was an asset when we went visiting. She could walk

into any home and within minutes she could grasp the dynamics of the household and figure out how to fit in. She was the one who made a game fun by adding another dimension. If we visited a place where there were girls, she suggested outrageous dress-ups, or played store with real money, or suggested they bake cupcakes and enlisted the aide of an older sibling who was allowed to turn on the oven.

She could organize anyone. Except Max. He wanted to be her friend but they might as well have come from different planets. He was hard to take anywhere. He couldn't seem to grasp limits and had no interest in playing with the other children so I ended up repeatedly grabbing him from the edge of disaster. After a few visits with him in tow the invitations to bring the kids petered out except from my dearest friends who were willing to endure constant interruptions from Max to have my company.

Max was a serious child. I had never heard him go off into gales of laughter until the day Pete brought home an old-fashioned Jack-in-the-Box. Max was at the hanging-onto-things-but-not-yet-walking stage. The toy was a large, brightly colored music box that played Pop Goes the Weasel. Pete set it on the coffee table in the living room and wound the crank.

Max was no more than a foot away from the toy. Linda was a couple of feet behind him. I stood in the doorway to the kitchen. We all jumped when a large, gaudy clown figure abruptly leaped out of the box. Max was so startled he fell backward and plunked down on the rug. He stared at the box. I expected him to cry. But he broke into wild peals of laughter, pulled himself up and said, "Again."

So Pete pushed the clown back in the box, closed the lid and turned the crank. Max hadn't figured out the tune yet so he was just as startled this time and again he collapsed in laughter. Pete replayed the tune a few more times. Every time the clown leaped out, Max cracked up and said, "Again." After that, whenever I sat down in the living room, Max crawled over to the toy box, pulled out the Jack-in-the-Box, dragged it over and plunked it on the table in front of me. I cranked it over and over just to hear him laugh.

Winters in Concord were long and harsh. The kids hated being bundled up in heavy snowsuits but the alternative was frostbite. So we stayed home a lot. Fortunately, my friend and neighbor Mary and I visited back and forth. She was a role model for the person I would have loved to be. Ten years my senior, she gave me the considerable compliment of treating me as her intellectual equal. She told me once I was "all of a piece," an expression she had picked up in England. She had graduated from Bennington, lived in London and been on her own for years before she married a fascinating man and decided to raise a family. Witty, she had a rare gift for seeing people with all their peculiarities and putting these perceptions into succinct comments.

One day she mentioned that Pete didn't really like women. She wasn't being critical. It was clear she didn't care one way or the other. It was just an offhand observation delivered in the same impartial way she might have said he had blue eyes.

Her comment flew around my mind pinging as it banged against stored bits of information like a well shot ball in a pinball game. I had always watched people's faces and tried to figure out what they were thinking. Her comment made me more watchful. I started listening for the undercurrents when Pete talked about or to women. I soon realized Mary was right. Then it slowly dawned on me that he didn't like women because he was afraid of them. This wasn't surprising with a mother like his who made him feel inadequate no matter what he did. I never did understand why he didn't stand up to her or assert his own rights when she was egregiously rude to him or why he became so angry and upset with me on the rare occasions when I confronted her. What was he afraid of? There was little she could do that could hurt him more than she already had.

33

After a few weeks with two sick children and gale winds that kept me housebound, I knew I was on the path to brain death when a friend who was married to a furniture designer asked if I would help her pass out hors d'oeuvres at a party to celebrate the opening of a new store. I was delighted. I got a baby sitter and drove into Cambridge. I was happily carrying around platter after platter of luscious food I didn't have to cook, smiling at all the adults and getting smiles and thanks in return. A scruffy-looking bearded man took a stuffed mushroom wrapped in bacon from my platter. He started to turn away then stopped abruptly and gaped at me with the goody poised in front of his mouth. What I had just said to the man played back like a recording in my mind, "Now say thank you," delivered in the automatic sing-song phrasing of a mother teaching a child good manners. Realizing immediately how silly this sounded, I said, "Sorry, I don't get out much," and giggled. The man glared at me. He probably didn't like his mother. He left shortly after.

I decided I had better get out more or confine my forays into the real world to movies, where I didn't have to speak to other adults.

Chapter 8

Pete had inherited his father's reliance on moving to fix problems. A friend intimately associated with Alcoholics Anonymous called this The Geographic Cure. By the time we had been married five years, we had moved three times and I could see he was getting restless again. I loved Concord and I wanted to stay there. I had good friends and a constructive outlet for my love of reading and writing. I was close to the end of the second semester of an accredited English course offered on the Harvard campus by the University of Massachusetts Extension. The course gave me an anchor, allowing me to create scenarios based on tangible problems I could solve. A succession of A grades made me feel I was capable of something more demanding than what I was doing.

When Pete had an unexpected shot at an art director's job with a top advertising agency in Philadelphia, I reluctantly agreed it was too big a chance to turn down. I had done a small amount of artwork in the years after Linda was born, even less after Max's birth and the move to Concord. Pete was now the primary wage earner and his desire to move into the world of big-time agencies made sense.

We made a quick trip to Philadelphia and rented a garage apartment in Chestnut Hill through one of those friend of a friend of a friend referrals that seemed to rent most garage apartments.

The agency had given Pete a wide time frame to start. I asked him to set his beginning date so I could take my final English Literature exam and get credit for the semester's work. He chose a date a week before my class ended. I was dismayed and protested. He said he hadn't paid attention to what I said about the timing of my final exam because it didn't seem all that important.

"It's important to me. You said they gave you a wide time frame for your move. Can't you just tell them you need to make your start date a week later?"

"What reason would I give them? My wife wanted to take an English exam? How the hell would I justify that? I gave them a start date and I'm not going to change it now."

I bugged him to the point where he finally snapped at me. He chanted a weird rhyme I had never heard before. "He who pays, says." He made "says" rhyme with "pays."

"Who made up that inane saying? It sounds like something you heard in grade school. And what's the point?"

He assumed his disgusted 'boy, are you immature' expression, sighed and said, "I didn't mind paying for English classes if frittering away your time reading and writing about old books made you happy, but *I* am the *"only one* making money in this family and the one with the job gets to make all the *important* decisions."

I felt equal measures of fury and dismay. "Why do you need to make me feel so worthless?"

"Why do *you* always have to make something simple into a complicated scenario?"

He turned away, walked into the kitchen and said, "When's dinner going to be ready? I'm hungry."

Chapter 9

Chestnut Hill was part of the city of Philadelphia but a long way from downtown. Max was nineteen months old when we moved from Concord. He watched Pete and me putting together the cribs. That evening, I found the large screwdriver we had been using under a blanket in his bed. He looked at me with wide eyes. I got the impression he thought I had some kind of magical insight into everything in the world because I found it without actually seeing it. I didn't tell him I recognized the shape under his blanket. With Max I needed every edge I could get. After that I checked his bed for anything he could use as a screwdriver.

At some point he noticed that the screwdriver slots in the tops of the long bolts attaching the side rails to the crib shifted side to side each time he shook the rail. What followed appeared to be a simple physics experiment. Shaking the side, he held his finger on top of the bolt and pressed down at different points in the screw's arc to see what would happen. He noticed a spot where pressure unscrewed the bolt in minute increments. He moved from side to side, methodically loosening both sides. In the middle of the night, a crash jolted us awake. The side of his crib was on the floor. When he offered to do the same thing to his sister's crib we conceded defeat. Pete made two bed frames six inches off the ground for the crib mattresses. The children's bedroom opened off ours and the hinges on their door made an ungodly screech. I didn't know if it was the fact he no longer felt he was sleeping inside a cage or the obvious unease he felt living in what he had decided was the middle of a forest but Max stayed in his room.

The carriage house was like a doll house on top of a four-car garage at the end of a sweeping, boxwood-lined driveway on two wooded acres in the center of Chestnut Hill. Small casement windows set in dormers looked out on a large greenhouse and the gable end and kitchen wing of a Georgian style brick mansion. The faint sounds of traffic seemed to come from another world.

For me, the most compelling plus in the move to Philadelphia was the increased distance from my supposedly dying mother-in-law, who looked healthier each time I saw her. When I described the apartment to her I stressed the small size. I should have known this wouldn't deter her.

Our first apartment in New York City was a large studio yet my mother-in-law showed up regularly with no advance warning. She never called before leaving Melrose; her phone calls were usually made from a booth on the Hutchinson River Parkway.

Death of a Salesman was a sensational play in its first New York run. Instantly a must-see, there was a long wait for tickets. We had bought balcony tickets four months earlier. The evening we were going to the play, Ada called from the Bronx River Parkway irritated that we hadn't been home when she tried to reach us half an hour earlier. She said she would be at our apartment within the hour. She hoped we had food—she was famished. Dismayed, I had looked at the near-empty refrigerator. We had planned to get deli sandwiches. We were meeting another couple at the theater.

I said, "What is she going to do while we're at the play? Maybe she can go to a movie."

Pete had retreated into cold withdrawal mode. "I'll give her my ticket."

"You know that doesn't make sense. Why can't you just tell her we had plans for this evening? She's going to hate the play. I don't think Arthur Miller is her style."

"I said I'll give her *my* ticket to the play because she's *my* mother."

I was careful not to say what I was thinking. I couldn't afford to get into a pissing contest about the merits of our mothers.

38

Ada accepted the play ticket without questioning that she had every right to it. Then not only did she hate *Death of a Salesman*, she declaimed in a loud voice during the play that she was horrified that any son would dare to talk to his father in such a nasty way. Her noisy ire was a constant since heated father-son arguments were a large part of the play's plot. All around us people kept shushing her. I would have loved to pretend I didn't know her but she turned her head and glared at me each time she delivered a scathing editorial comment. She complained bitterly about the terrible play all the way home. Pete never got to see the play but I couldn't work up much sympathy for him.

We only lived in Chestnut Hill for five months but Ada managed to drop in on us without warning twice then complained because we didn't have a comfortable bed for her. She hinted that she expected Pete and me to give her our bed. I ignored her hints and stressed that the children got up all night long with nightmares ever since we had moved and would cry if I wasn't immediately available. I only felt a little bit guilty.

I resisted having a third child but Pete was relentless. The women I counted as close friends all lived too far away to offer me a sounding board. We wrote back and forth but discussing my strong reservations about having another child was something that still went against accepted norms in the fifties. I needed to discuss it face to face so I could read their expressions.

Once again, I was caught in a situation where I was dependent on Pete. He stayed reasonable, pointing out that the two children we had didn't get along at all. He said this was too much like his own childhood. He was certain a third child would improve the dynamics and make us into a better family.

Having been the middle child of three for most of my childhood, I knew this position was no guarantee of all-around bliss for any of the siblings. What if a third child acted like Max? Then there would be two kids competing with Linda for my attention.

I finally agreed anything was better than the bad feeling between the two we had. There was no hope of a third child in the tiny garage apartment so I set out to find a house. Ever hopeful, I looked in Chestnut Hill and also checked out the towns on the Paoli train line. I wanted a place with frequent and accessible trains. So did everyone else and they had more money than we did so the price of houses close to the city was too high.

Half of the men in the art department in Pete's advertising agency came from California. Most of these former West Coasters lived in Levittown. They thought a tedious hour and a quarter car commute was normal. To them trains were weird.

After months of trying to house-hunt with two small kids in tow, I agreed to move to Levittown. The house was great. Four bedrooms and two full baths felt pretty luxurious after a carriage house.

The other art directors and their families were used to the casual entertainment style they had enjoyed in California. They instigated impromptu parties to celebrate the smallest event or non-event. I loved this. Coming from a home where no one was ever invited to share a meal with the family, I realized I'd somehow ended up with a genetic mix much different from my parents. I loved having people underfoot and thoroughly enjoyed feeding crowds. An added plus, there was always someone at the parties who thought Max was delightful.

At a party with a bunch of these art directors and their wives, one of the men went off on a long-winded gripe about an account executive who thought he was an art director and insisted on changing every layout before he would show it to the client. I was listening, trying to figure out who they were discussing. I was probably frowning, something I inadvertently do when I think. My hostess, a nice woman I had seen at parties before but didn't know well, assumed I had no idea what the man was talking about. She had been an art buyer at a small agency. She started explaining what happened each time something in the layout of a print ad was changed even if it was just the size of the type.

It took me a few minutes to grasp why she felt the need to explain this to me. When the import of her words sunk in, sweat gathered on my brow and under my arms. She thought I was baffled by what the men were saying. Feeling sick, I wondered when and why I had allowed a large part of myself to be erased and had become *only* someone's wife and the mother of his children.

What was I doing? When had I become the reflection of other people's perception of my role? The men were animated and involved, the women the same way. Both were talking about what mattered most in their lives. I was interested in both conversations but there was no cross-over.

My hostess looked puzzled. Her voice trailed off. "Are you all right? Can I get you a glass of water?"

"I worked in advertising. I used to *do* what they're talking about. Pete and I met at art school." My voice was too abrupt. The buzz of women's voices halted.

My hostess looked embarrassed. "I'm so sorry. I didn't know."

"There's no reason why you would know. We never talk about anything except children and food. I was just jolted to realize all I am now is Pete's wife and the mother of two kids with another one on the way."

My hostess looked around at the other women. I could see her assessing how much damage control she needed to cover up my unflattering comment about the women's roles. Hoping for some vote of assent, I turned to the woman next to me. "What did *you* do before you married?"

"Went to college." She was mumbling. She looked trapped. Some part of me tried to tell myself to shut up but I blundered on. "What was your major?"

She looked chagrined. "I didn't finish my first year so I never declared a major. Jamie wanted to get married so..." She shrugged with a *what could I do* expression on her face.

I asked the rest of the women the same questions. Even the women who had finished college seemed to accept their lives as their husband's helpmate.

One woman finally asked me, "What did *you* want to do that's better than bringing up a happy family?" I looked around and realized the women were looking at me with pity.

"Establish a career. Find out who I am before I spread myself so thin I don't have the time or energy to explore what I'm capable of doing on my own."

This statement was as popular as a fart.

The artists in Pete's circle liked to party. And drink. Fortunately, most of them also loved to eat so this usually worked out. At the next party, our host had been fighting with his wife since he got out of bed so he skipped dinner and was drunk by the time dessert was served. Like many of the art directors, he freelanced on the side. Revisions to a full-page newspaper ad were marked in red on a comprehensive drawing tacked on his drawing board next to a pad of layout bond paper. I was looking at this as I polished off the last of my dessert. My host floated by muttering about how hard it was going to be to finish the revision with a hangover.

Swallowing my last bite of key lime pie, I said, "When's it due?"

"Ten o'clock tomorrow." Snickering, he said, "My wife says you claim to be an artist. You wanna do it?" This was so slurred, I couldn't be sure this was what he really said. He passed out on the couch shortly after that so I couldn't double-check.

The women were clumped on the other side of the room discussing bed-wetting. This wasn't an issue in my household so I figured what the hell, sat down at the drawing board and did the revision. He could use it or not. All he was out was a sheet of good bond paper. Men stopped by and watched. It was obvious I knew what I was doing. The revisions marked on the initial layout were written in an artist's short-hand code.

One man laughed and said, "I'd love to be here tomorrow when Randy wakes up with a hangover, drags himself over to his drawing board and tries to figure out when and how he finished the comp. And how he did such a good job."

I glowed. It felt great to do something tangible that had a beginning and an end.

Another man grinned. "Let's tell him he did it. That'll really freak him out."

"Nah. He'll just get drunk every time he has a freelance job to finish hoping he'll wake up and find it all done."

The first man turned to me. "How about it? We could have his wife call you. And you could wait until he passes out and slip into the house and finish the comp."

The idea was entertaining. They were half serious. Pete had told me about some of the elaborate practical jokes the artists carried out. "It's okay by me but I'm not sure his wife would agree. I gather Randy is a bear when he has a hangover."

Regret in his voice, the second man said, "Yeah, I guess it's not a good idea. Randy doesn't need any more reasons to tie one on."

Pete came home early the following Thursday. Max and Linda were already fed and in their pajamas. It was a little early for bedtime but Pete liked to have them in bed when he got home. I closed the book I had been reading to them. "Say goodnight to your dad, kids. I'll finish the story tomorrow."

"Let them stay up. I have to take a few photos of them for work. You can go to the store as soon as we eat. I'll put them to bed."

This unexpected help from Pete was a nice surprise and I made the best of it. I dawdled. Buying groceries without the children had become one of the high points of my week. I tried not to dwell on this sorry commentary on my life.

When I got home, Pete was up in his studio working. I smelled turpentine, not an odor I had smelled recently. Pete had planned to be a painter before we married. He wasn't alone. The art floor at his agency was full of wannabe painters just as the copy floor was filled with writers who dreamed of writing the Great American Novel. These longings were soon eclipsed by the Great American Dream of wife, three children, house, car and enough money to make it all happen.

After the groceries were put away, I went up to see what he was painting. He said it was just something for work so I went to bed.

He needed the car the next day because the paint on the canvas was still wet. That was when he said the agency was having a show of art-work in the company gallery and the head art director had insisted he enter something. The painting was already in the car and he said he had to hurry so I didn't see it.

The show's opening was that Friday. I got a sitter and drove into town. In the late fifties there were two ways to get from Levittown to Center City, Philadelphia. Either wend your way down Roosevelt Boulevard with a traffic light at every corner or take the Burlington Bristol Bridge into New Jersey then drive down Route 130 and across a second bridge back into Pennsylvania. Neither way was good.

When I went into the gallery, a cluster of people stood staring at Pete's picture. It hung in a conspicuous spot. Mostly white paint applied with a palette knife, it had a sign below it saying WET PAINT. It took a while to work my way to the front of the people. When I did, I was stunned. Pete had caught the essence of our two children's personalities and relationship. Linda was relaxed and appeared to be pleased. Max was wide-eyed and looked worried. His right hand was clamped over his mouth.

The man next to me said, "I wonder who these children are. What a powerful picture. I get the sense there's a story here. That poor little boy looks frightened."

Chapter 10

I was thrilled when my neighbor invited Linda and two-year-old Max down to her yard to play on the large swing set her husband had spent the last week setting up. She promised she would stay next to the swing set and supervise. They lived two houses away down the hill in the direction of the creek on the far side of the road circling our sub-division. I kept going into my backyard to check on Max. It looked as though every kid in the development was playing on the swing set. Linda was on the glider laughing or on one of the swings. Max was observing from a perch on one of the crossbars bracing the side. He wasn't a group player but he loved to climb. The neighbor waved at me each time I went out. Her husband sat with her at the small patio table. He looked pleased with himself, like a king surveying his fiefdom. He nodded to me with a satisfied expression. The scene looked like an ad for the Sears outdoor section, everyone's idea of the perfectly equipped backyard in the suburbs.

I was folding clothes from the dryer when someone pounded on the front door. Alarmed, I yanked it open. The swing set man loomed in the doorway quivering with fury. He clutched Max's hand. Next to the man's bulk, Max looked like a small doll. Clearly terrified, his eyes were like enormous lapis marbles so wide open I could see their inner curve. Each time Max tried to pull his hand loose, the swing set man yanked him so hard his feet swung off the ground. The man sputtered, spraying me with beer-tinged saliva. His voice rose with each garbled word. I felt like clapping my hands over my ears. I couldn't figure out what he was saying.

I didn't care how big and mean the man was, I wasn't going to let some hulking bully yank Max around. I reached over my pregnant belly, put my hands under Max's armpits and tried to lift him. I could see the man's eyes shifting. He was trying to decide whether he really wanted to have a tug-of-war with a pregnant woman. I looked him in the eye trying to out-mean him. He finally let go of Max's hand but compensated by leaning into the doorway and shaking his fist at him. Max flinched each time the man came close. I was tempted to step back but was afraid the man would just follow me into the house.

I realized Linda was cowering on the sidewalk behind him. I held up my right hand in front of his face in classic cop-stop style and startled the burly man into a brief pause in his still unintelligible tirade.

"Excuse me, my little girl's trying to get past you."

He half-turned and reached down as though he planned to grab her. She shot past him with an evasive maneuver that would have made any quarterback proud and stationed herself behind my left knee. I took advantage of the break in his abuse. "I can see you're upset but I still don't know why. Can you speak more slowly?"

"Yeah. YOUR DAMN KID TOOK APART THE SWING SET IT TOOK ME A WEEK TO SET UP. Did you hear me that time?"

"He did what?" Before he could answer, I said, "Are you sure the swing set wasn't defective?"

"No way, lady. Sears don't sell defective stuff. "

I tried to sound reasonable. "How could a little kid take apart a swing set if there wasn't something wrong with it?"

Before I could stop him, Max said, "Like the cribs." I gave him a warning squeeze but he was impossible to silence once he started on an explanation.

The man kept yelling, Max kept explaining how he did it and I tried to talk above them both. Now that both kids were safe I was fighting not to laugh. I concentrated on keeping a thoughtful frown on my face but my chest bounced with suppressed glee. Max stopped telling the man how he dismantled the swing set and looked at my face. He was clearly confused. He had no sense of the ridiculous. I tried to tuck him against my shoulder but he

46

flipped his head out of my grasp and reared back so he could see my face. He looked at me with an intent expression. I tried to give him a "don't talk" warning with my face alone but he didn't seem to be able to read body language.

The man began to wind down. "What your kids need is a good beating. You're a disgrace to the neighborhood." He gestured at the black VW beetle in the driveway. "How can you drive around in that Kraut excuse for a car? Ain't you got no pride?" He swung back to me. "I don't want to see none of your kids in my yard. Not her," He jabbed a finger at Linda then at Max, "and not that devil kid you're holding there. If I see one a them anywhere near my yard, I'll give them a good beating myself."

Linda stalked off as soon as I closed the front door and said, "I was having fun. Now I won't have anyone to play with. All the kids are going to be playing down on the swing set. Max ruins everything for me. I wish you never borned him." Her voice was bitter. She stomped down the hall wailing as though her world was about to end and slammed her bedroom door behind her.

Chapter 11

I insisted the kids had to spend an hour in their room every day after lunch. They didn't nap any more but I needed to put my feet up. I was out cold as soon as I was prone. With a baby due in a few weeks it was a struggle to get off the couch when the buzzer on the stove went off. I dragged myself into the kitchen, punched the button to stop the abrasive noise and turned on the burner under the kettle. I needed a large cup of tea to get through the afternoon. I didn't hear the kids. There was a hook on the outside of their door and their room was baby-proof so I knew they were safe.

I put a tea bag in my empty cup, waddled back to their room, unlatched the hook and opened the bedroom door. Yawning, I looked around the room. Linda was sitting on her bed but I didn't see Max. I slid open the closet door and looked inside. No Max. Linda looked sullen and guilty and the high sliding window over her bed was open. Moving my off-center bulk as quickly as I could, I ran to the window and craned my head out. "Where's Max?"

She shrugged. "He went out the window. It's not my fault." She cringed when I whipped around and glared at her. Her bed was under the window and the opening was so far above the bed she would have had to hoist him up for him to crawl out.

"When? Why didn't you call me?" I shrieked this as I was stumbling to the front door. I walked around the outside of the house shouting Max's name. I couldn't see him. I didn't expect him to answer but I yelled anyway. I checked the car and the garage. No child in either one.

Linda came out of the front door. "Your tea kettle's making noise." I pushed past her and turned off the burner. I called neighbors and the police. No one had seen him. The police took his description and my phone number and said they would put this on their radio. My neighbor across the street brought her baby over and said she would stay with Linda and answer the phone. I drove around the streets in my neighborhood stopping and asking anyone outside if they had seen a small boy wandering around. I gave them my phone number and asked them to call me or the police if they saw Max.

People were nice. Losing a child aroused atavistic terror in every parent. Having alerted at least one person on each of the surrounding streets, I tackled the wooded strip Max had asked to explore each time I drove past. I parked at the foot of the hill and went down the slippery bank to a mucky area referred to on local maps as a creek. There may have been a constantly running creek there when this area bordered a field of wheat but now it was just a strip of slimy mud with the occasional glimmer of a narrow meandering rivulet of sudsy water. It stunk. Thick stands of skunk cabbage still flourished in the deep shade under sumac and wild cherry trees. Ratty elderberry bushes bent toward the open spots where sun peeked through.

I caught movement on the edge of my vision. The tip of a hairless tail disappeared behind a rock. Too large for a mouse. Too small and fast moving for an opossum. I shuddered. It had to be a rat. Would it attack a small child? What if it had a nest of baby rats to protect? It was April. Did rats have young in the spring like deer and foxes? Max would want to pick up a baby rat if he saw one. Did they carry rabies like the local skunks?

It was hard to keep my footing. What if Max slipped and fell? He could have cracked his head against the rock where the rat went. Someone or something had been walking here earlier. Skunk cabbage leaves had been broken in a wavering path. I yanked a dead branch off a skeletal wild cherry tree and flailed it back and forth crushing everything in front of me. I had to get down to the bare mud to see if there were footprints. Oh God. Was he still wearing his shoes? I tried to picture his room. Were there shoes on the floor? I couldn't remember. My brain flopped from bad thought to worse. Why didn't I dress Max in red today? Or yellow? Why did I pick his green shirt? Attacking the stands of strong-smelling greenery left me with wet, muddy shoes and a rotten stench that clung to my baggy maternity pants but no little boy or even footprints.

I finally got to the iron pipe where the creek went under the road. It was too small for Max to squeeze into and covered with sturdy mesh that hadn't been tampered with. I had to retrace my steps and follow the creek in the other direction. This time I slipped and fell. Close to full term with a very large baby throwing me off balance I had to turn sideways and crawl on my knees to get back on my feet. My black pants were now stained with brown mud. The bottom end of the creek bed had an iron pipe slightly larger than the one at the top and was just as carefully sealed with heavy steel mesh. I clawed my way up the bank and hurried down the road to the place where I had left my car.

More and more frightened I went back to the house to see if the police had called. My neighbor shook her head. I had been hunting for Max for at least forty-five minutes now. He could have climbed out shortly after I fell asleep. I tried to find out from Linda but she said she didn't know. She defined time by when I fed her and put her to bed.

I debated calling Pete. He would want to know. But he was thirty miles away and commuted in a car pool. There wouldn't be anything he could do except worry himself sick and tie up the phone with calls every few minutes. I was torn between practical kindness and resentment. They were *his* kids, too. Why should *I* be the only one going crazy with fear? But I squelched my less charitable impulses. I knew he would be helping hunt and as frantic as I was if he were here.

I dashed out to the car and drove over the same few streets. I even stopped at the noisy stone-crushing plant where the two main roads intersected. No one had seen a very small boy in a green jersey. The two men working there looked at me with disapproval. What kind of woman loses her child?

I would have to call Pete. Maybe he could talk the man who was driving this week to leave early.

When I went back to find out if my neighbor had gotten any calls, she insisted I stop long enough for a cup of tea and suggested I change my clothes. I knew she was right. I was so exhausted by now I was afraid I might black out and crash into something when I got back on the road. I pulled on my other pair of maternity pants and gulped down a cup of sweet milky tea.

I lurched and spilled tea down my fresh clothes when the phone rang. I grabbed it and squeaked out a hello. A hesitant voice said, "Uh, ma'am, do you have a little boy..." I heard his voice asking someone a question then he spoke into the phone again, "I think his name is Maxwell?" This last was clearly a question. Not for the first time, I wished we had named our son John or Ed or Dan. Anything normal.

Max was at the drugstore I used. The one with the jars of pretzel sticks and lollipops and a marble soda fountain flanked by stools that went round and round with a satisfying squeak. The place where I got my pre-natal vitamins and never bought Linda or Max any of the teeth-rotting goodies they coveted. Max was sitting on one of the round stools drinking the last of what looked like a strawberry soda. When he saw me he burst into tears. The drug store manager and stock boy assumed he was crying with joy at the sight of his long lost mother. They both had goofy smiles on their faces until Max clutched the soda with a death grip and shrieked, "Don't take my soda. They said I could have it."

The druggist looked at me with suddenly cold, judgmental eyes as I paid for the soda, three lollipops, four pretzel sticks and a pack of Dentine gum. I thanked him for keeping Max safe. He had the grace to apologize for not calling earlier. "He told me his name but I figured he was too little to talk well because I couldn't figure out what he said his first name was. The last name was confusing enough. We tried every spelling we could and finally hit on one that looked like it might be pronounced like the name he kept saying. But the first name was so odd we figured he got the whole name wrong. What kind of a name *is* Maxwell?"

"A family name that seems to carry a curse."

Chapter 12

Max was two and a half when his brother Seth was born. He wasn't impressed. "Why's he so little?" He watched me change the baby's diaper and shuddered. "Yuck." He tried to hand Seth one of his trucks. I grabbed it before it dropped on his brother's head and explained Seth was too little to play with toys. Max frowned in disgust then delivered his final opinion. "Why didn't you bring home a bigger one? This one can't do anything." There was a long pause. "He can't even talk."

Linda watched Seth with interest. When he began to respond and smile, she sat next to his cradle, played with his fingers with a delighted expression on her face and made him laugh. Max watched her and brooded. He adored Linda, did anything she suggested without question and didn't tattle on her even when her instructions got him in trouble. She played with him because he was the only child available now that they were banned from the house on the corner but she made it clear he was a poor excuse for a *real* playmate. "You're not doing it right," came from the playroom all day long, delivered in a frustrated shriek.

Seth was easy and rewarding. Guilt nudged me each time I realized how profoundly grateful I was he wasn't another Max. This spurred me to compensate by giving Max extra attention. Each time I saw or heard something I particularly liked, I shared it with him. Or tried to. One evening when the stars were amazingly vivid, I carried him to the picture window so we could look at them.

He asked me what made them light up and why they didn't fall out of the sky. I said, "Hot gasses? Maybe they're too light to fall?" He heard the question in my voice and looked disappointed. I tried to explain my point of view. "I see stars as something beautiful, like a picture I love. I don't really care what they're made of, how they got where they are or why they stay there."

He turned and looked at my eyes. I wondered if he thought I didn't know about stars because my eyes were broken. He often stared at my face as though there were something wrong with me. He looked at his father the same way. We baffled him as much as he baffled us. He was clearly intelligent. I assumed he didn't understand gravity but he *had* figured out objects didn't stay up in the air by themselves. He had a large vocabulary and he used words well. He stared at the pages when I read to him and knew if I left out a word. I sometimes got the impression he was reading along with me but assumed he had a good memory for patterns. Two-and-a-half-year-olds can't read. His sister had just turned four. She had figured out that the octagonal red signs at the street corners said Stop but that might have been because I always said, "Stop," when I got to them.

I knew Max understood everything I said when I told him what I expected from him. I stuck to simple things. Stay out of the street. Respect other people's belongings. Don't climb on the roof or hang from the gutters. Eat what's on your plate without saying "yuck." Don't pick your nose, or scratch your bottom, or play with your penis in the living room or outside. Say please and thank you. Don't help yourself to candy when you're visiting someone. If they offer you candy, never take more than two pieces even if it's your favorite kind. Don't sass adults even if you think they're stupid. Try to keep your face from showing what you're really thinking if it isn't polite. The reason for each item was explained. This took a long time because Max debated each rule and demanded exact parameters. Then he ignored every rule unless it was what he wanted to do anyway.

He became convinced he was being cheated by his brother. He didn't understand why so he did what he could to even the score. He claimed every toy brought into the house for Seth. Baby toys like rattles, cloth books and soft animals ended up missing. I found them under his bed. Frustrated, I asked him why he took them. He didn't answer—or stop taking them. I finally just checked under his bed and in his closet to restock Seth's highchair tray and playpen a few times a day. Each time Max saw the reclaimed objects he stared at Seth and then at me with a venomous expression that chilled me.

One day he came into the kitchen with peppermint breath. It wasn't hard to figure out why. Pete periodically tried to stop smoking, stashed mints in his jacket pockets and then forgot they were there when he started smoking again. I propped my hands on my hips and asked Max why he had been going through his dad's pockets. His eyes popped open. Frantic, he looked around to see who had given him away then stared at me with a spooked expression on his face when he realized we were alone. I was feeding into his belief that I had magical powers. The familiar guilt cropped up but I felt at such a disadvantage with Max because I couldn't follow his thought processes, I was willing to ignore the guilt and go against all my beliefs of fairness if it would help keep him safe. Maybe if he thought I knew everything he did he might think twice before he did it. So far I had no reason to believe this but I was eternally hopeful.

I noticed each time Seth made a gain in function Max lost one. By the time Seth first pulled up to a standing position in his playpen and gave a triumphant crow of delight Max was barely speaking. Something was eating at him. Max watched Seth with his eyes hooded and his mouth turned down. I couldn't decide if his expression meant anger, profound depression, or both. My heart hurt to see this strange but vibrant boy shrinking inside himself and becoming non-verbal. I had to get help. We didn't have a pediatrician so I made an appointment with the general practitioner who took care of all our medical needs. He was smart, nice and he liked Max. He spent an hour alone with him then he had the nurse take him out to the waiting room and called me into his office.

"There's nothing wrong with your son. I wish I had kids that personable and bright. His vocabulary is better than mine. He asked me how all my equipment worked and then listened to my answers. Stop worrying and just enjoy him."

Thinking the doctor could help was stupid on my part. One-on-one encounters with someone who would listen to him were Max's forte. I thanked the doctor and drove home more worried than I was before. The pediatrician who took care of him when we lived in Concord was the only one who seemed to understand there was something intrinsically different about Max. I called his office in Massachusetts. He had just had a cancellation for the following day so I set up an appointment. At two o'clock the following morning, I carried the three sleeping kids out to the VW beetle and drove to Melrose, the town north of Boston where the pediatrician lived. My mother-in-law still lived there and we went back and forth often enough so the kids were used to long car rides. The drive to Melrose usually took six or seven hours. Being cooped up in a small car with three children under five would have seemed to be an invitation to misery somewhere between purgatory and hell. But timing was everything. All three slept most of the way.

The pediatrician checked Max physically, listened with a bemused expression when the small boy explained what made the stethoscope work then laughed when Max asked if he could have two lollipops without getting a shot first. He buzzed his nurse.

"Liz, can you please give this young man two lollipops?"

Max cut in. "Without shots?"

"Right. No shots please."

The doctor watched Max take the nurse's hand without protest. "Amazing." He indicated the stethoscope tucked into his pocket. "I've been using this thing for so long I'd almost forgotten how it works. So tell me exactly why you dragged your son all the way to Melrose."

"He's stopped speaking in sentences at home. He's sad, angry and he often seems frightened."

He looked at Max's old chart. "He was unusually articulate for a one-and-a-half-year-old when I last saw him. What do *you* think is causing him to regress?"

"I have a new baby boy. He's ten months old now. Linda obviously loves the baby but she can't stand poor Max. I'm guessing he thought that her contempt was just part of her make-up. Now he knows it's aimed at him."

"What about your husband?"

I was torn. I was raised to believe it was wrong to discuss family problems with outsiders. But I needed help. "He's never been comfortable with Max."

"What does your husband do?"

"He's withdrawn and overly critical with Max and always easily affectionate with Seth. He tries to like Max. I can see he knows he's being unfair but he can't stop himself."

"That must be hard on Max."

I nodded. "He looks devastated when Pete yells at him then turns around and hugs Seth. When Pete leaves, Max watches Seth with a menacing expression as though Seth were something he hadn't ordered and plans to send back."

"Menacing how?"

"He looks angry and coldly detached at the same time. I sometimes feel he's measuring Seth with his eyes to figure out where to stuff his body." I hunched my shoulders and hugged my elbows.

The doctor nodded. I had been hoping he would tell me this was ridiculous.

"How are *you* doing?"

I wasn't used to being asked how I was doing. It took me a second to decide what to say. "I feel like I'm living under a curse. Sometimes it's hard to breathe. Max seems to suck up all the air in the house. I never know what he's going to do next so I'm always in a knot." I could feel my voice thickening. I looked down at my clenched hands. "Sometimes I hate my life."

He shook his head. "You've got to get help. That's no way to live. I don't know who to refer you to in your area but a pediatrician I've known since we were residents lives in Philadelphia." He flipped open an address book, wrote something on a piece of paper and handed it to me. "Give him a call. He'll know who you can go to for help and give you a referral."

Chapter 13

A month after I got back from Massachusetts, we moved into a house in Center City, Philadelphia. Tired of being stuck out in the suburbs, I had convinced Pete to look at houses downtown. He was weary of the long drive and time restraints of a car pool with four other men in it so it was not hard to convince him. Five months earlier we had found and bought a house in bad shape on Pine Street, a twenty-minute walk from his office. During the period of gutting and rebuilding, I went into town once or twice a week to keep track of the progress and attack odd jobs no one else wanted to do.

The mother of our favorite baby sitter took care of the kids the days I was gone. I didn't get the impression she had a sense of humor but her daughter was kind, endlessly patient and liked Max so I decided the baby sitter's mother knew how to raise children. She had all three children bathed, fed and in pajamas by the time I got home. I loved this. Linda and Seth were happy. Max looked haunted and began having nightmares.

I knew he didn't want to move. He wanted every day to be the same. Any change in routine made him edgy. So he followed me around all day long. I literally couldn't move without tripping over him. He vibrated neediness. I did everything I could to reassure him. I read to him, encouraged him to talk even if he asked the same question repeatedly and didn't seem to listen to my reply. I knew nothing would have any effect on his anxiety short of cancelling the move. This wasn't a new problem. He always tracked my every move if he sensed his routine was about to be altered. He even had a problem with weekends and holidays.

Linda resented his single-minded insistence on having my undivided attention as much as I did, no matter how hard I tried to stifle my feelings. I liked being alone, I liked being able to read an article or a book. Linda could be with me, and play happily without intruding on my every thought. She was good company; she seemed to have an innate grasp of boundaries that Max completely lacked. He felt every person and every object was an extension of him and should be immediately available to him.

I looked forward to my days in Philadelphia overseeing the house renovations. No matter what I did, it was peaceful to move around without Max attached to my side.

We wanted to leave the salmon brick party wall in the new house cleaned off and without plaster. The Italian mason refused to chip off the old plaster. He wouldn't even let his helper do it. So it fell to me. He did agree to re-point it but only if I promised not to tell anyone he did it. He said his reputation would be ruined if it got around.

Chipping plaster off salmon brick was a difficult, tedious job. The brick was soft. A too vigorous whack on the cold chisel left a permanent divot. At the end of a day, my hands were cramped and achy, my ears rang from the repeated clang of metal on metal and I hacked up brick and cement dust too fine to be stopped by my mask. But I was happier doing this than I was spending endless days cooped up in the house with Max dogging every step and quivering with his impossible to meet needs. I sometimes wondered what it would be like to raise just Linda and Seth. Like Max, they were fascinating. I felt privileged to watch them evolve but every time I tried to do something special with either of them, Max's never-ending insistence on possessing my undivided time ruined the experience for everyone.

Shortly after we moved into town, I heard Linda yelling. "The devil's going to get you if you don't stop that."

I walked into the living room where they were playing. Linda glared at Max, her face flushed, her hands firmly planted on her hips. Max looked frightened. Shoulders pulled inward and head tucked down as far as it could go, he looked like a threatened turtle that couldn't pull his head inside the shell.

"Where did you hear about devils, Linda?"

Both children whirled and faced me. They looked as though they had just been caught robbing a bank. Linda pursed her lips. Her head bobbed side to side. "The baby sitter said Max had the devil inside him. She prayed to make the devil go out of him. But it didn't work. He still takes all my best things."

She was a gifted mimic. I recognized the cadence of the baby sitter's speech.

"Devils don't exist, Linda. They're just something people made up a long time ago to scare everyone else into being good."

Linda's eyes got that opaque look I would see frequently when she started kindergarten next fall. The "what do *you* know—you're just my mother" look.

"He is *too* real. The baby sitter showed us a picture of the devil in her Bible. He was stabbing people. And they got really deaded when he stuck them with his sword. She goes to church every Sunday so *she* knows about devils."

I was furious with the baby sitter but I knew talking to a religious zealot who believed she knew the only road to heaven was a waste of time. It was a moot point anyway; I would never see her again.

From Linda's guilty reaction when I overheard her talking about devils, I knew she wouldn't have told me what was going on even if I had known what to ask. I was irritated with myself to realize I so easily assumed Max's increasing anxiety was caused only by the threat of moving. I had noticed that the baby sitter was a neat freak but hadn't bothered to consider how she would deal with a three-year-old who was essentially uncontrollable. I opted to ignore how she was keeping Max under control because I loved coming home to peace and folded clothes.

Chapter 14

I was thrilled with the move. Downtown Philadelphia with its bustle, its easy to use public transportation system, its sidewalks that went somewhere I wanted to go and its child-friendly parks full of interesting people was the real world. The world I wanted to experience. No matter how many bathrooms it had, a tract house thirty miles away from town was my idea of hell.

As soon as we were settled enough so we could all leave the house fully clothed, I followed up on the Melrose pediatrician's referral and made an appointment with his doctor friend. His office was up near Temple University. It was a hard place to find. I was at my wit's end by the time I found a place to park.

Max was his usual hard to control self. He wasn't interested in the toys. He wanted to find out why the three-way table lamp wouldn't turn from on to off and kept trying to turn the switch backward. I had Seth on one hip because there was no place to put him down. Nothing I said had any effect on Max. The doctor watched this with a disgusted frown on his face.

He examined Max then said, "What the boy needs is firm discipline." He gave me a referral to a group of child psychiatrists in West Philadelphia. "This group is the best I've run into. I think you *both* need help."

Ten days later, a psychiatrist, a psychologist and a social worker at the Child Study Center in West Philadelphia questioned me and gave Max an exhaustive battery of tests. It was a slow process. I kept checking my watch. Linda and Seth were home with a baby sitter from the nurse's registry. The nurses were capable and expensive. This was going to be a macaroni and cheese and tuna casserole week.

The male psychiatrist did most of the talking. "Do you have *any* idea what Max's IQ is?" He sounded affronted. As though I had just flunked a simple parenting exam.

I hated it when someone discovered how bright Max was and immediately assumed his inability to behave the way they thought such a gifted child should was the direct result of bad mothering. I clumped them together as the "If you only..." people. Add your own ending. Some form of "taught proper discipline" usually headed the list—it was certainly my mother-in-law's favorite. "Spent more constructive time with him" was a close second.

It was hard enough dealing with the guilt I felt on my own each time I got angry with Max because I couldn't begin to understand why he repeated the same destructive behavior over and over. I didn't need these allegedly top-notch experts starting out with an accusatory statement. I had hoped they would understand that what I did or didn't do seemed to have no effect on Max's actions. But they never quite got that aspect of his personality.

I tried to keep my frustration out of my voice but I didn't do too well. "No, I don't know what his IQ is. And I don't want to know." This was clearly the wrong response. They looked at each other with identical expressions. As though they were all thinking, is this one stupid or what?

I was defensive. "Look, Max's IQ isn't the issue. Whether it's high or low, he's out of sync with the rest of the world. He's bright enough to see something's wrong with his understanding of what's going on around him—God knows he's been told often enough—but he doesn't know what it is or how to fix it. He believes anything he's told because he can't imagine the mind set of a person who would lie to him. This makes him easy to bully. He's small for his age. Imagine how irritating it is to any aggressive child when this kid half his size starts to talk and sound like a college professor. This is making Max frustrated and angry, interfering with his development and screwing up the rest of the family to the point where no one is happy. All I need to know is whether you can help him learn how to cope successfully in the real world."

There was a pause. They looked at me then at each other and then back to me. The psychiatrist said, "We'll have to get together for another meeting before we can diagnose Max's problems accurately and help you begin to solve what's going wrong and why. Doing this will require a lengthy commitment of time and money from both you and your husband. We also have to meet with Max's father before we decide if Max can be admitted to our program."

This turned out to be a problem. Pete told me the kids were my job. He wouldn't have time for meetings. He would have to use any free time he had to take on freelance jobs if I planned to put Max in a private school. However Pete finally agreed to a meeting with the three experts.

He was stone-faced and withdrawn. His body language indicated his contempt for the whole process. I was anxious. He could be sarcastic. I knew he had no use for people who couldn't cope on their own, who "stared at their own navels" as he phrased it. I was never sure where this contempt for people who were interested in exploring their own and other people's thought processes came from but it pervaded his thinking and his consistently negative reactions. I learned from other sources that his mother had a severe nervous breakdown and was hospitalized when his brother died. Pete never alluded to it so it may have had nothing to do with his ongoing put-down of anyone who dealt with mental issues. Fortunately, he didn't say much to the staff interviewing him and just shrugged what could have been assent or dissent when asked a question. I hoped the experts didn't notice the contemptuous curl to his lip that accompanied his shrugs but he made little effort to hide it so I assumed they hadn't missed it.

I wasn't sure what the admission process entailed. I was cynical enough to think that making sure my husband was willing to pay the tuition was an important factor. He agreed to this and Max was accepted to start in what they called The Normal Nursery in September. Unfortunately, that was two months away.

Our house was in the middle of the twenty-five hundred block of Pine Street in what was called Center City, Philadelphia. It was a pretty block with a solid row of three-story brick row houses on the south side, a row of new town houses with garages on the ground floor on the north side. This row of town houses was flanked by a coal yard on the end of the block toward the Schuylkill River. Many of the older houses in this part of town still had coal furnaces so there were trucks going in and out all day long. It was hard to keep window sills free of grainy black coal dust but I figured a little grit was a good trade-off for being in the city.

The houses on our side of Pine Street were built around 1850 by the owners of a long-gone lace factory on the Schuylkill River and occupied initially by Irish immigrants who were skilled lace-makers. I gather this was an insular group. Our next-door neighbor was the third generation in the same house. She still rented the property and spoke with a slight brogue. There was an Irish bar on the corner with a lady's entrance on the side street so no lady had to walk past the bar itself. I didn't know if this was to protect the ladies' sensibilities or the drinker's identities.

Brick must have been cheap in the mid-eighteen-hundreds. Everything was brick: sidewalks, houses and even the few remaining outhouses. It was pretty but I wouldn't recommend walking on a brick sidewalk in bare feet in the summer. The steps were two or three slabs of white marble in diminishing lengths laid on top of each other. The marble was scratched and worn down in the middle of each step by more than a hundred years of tromping feet. The old woman next door dragged her thickened body outside each morning, sprinkled cleanser on her steps then crouched with groans and cracking joints and scoured them. She had an endless supply of tent-like cotton dresses.

Flesh-colored cotton stockings were rolled down below swollen ankles and spilled over the tops of leather slippers so old it was impossible to picture the original color. She had the red-veined face of a serious drinker and the thick, purple-blotched legs of someone with poor circulation who sits a lot.

She mumbled about the decline of standards on the block then looked meaningfully at my gray, dirt-embedded steps. I finally scoured them and then was so intimidated by the whiteness; I hated to walk on them. I scoured the steps three days in a row then decided that gray was fine with me. My neighbor was a kind woman. She gave me credit for trying and conceded you had to be born in Philadelphia to care about white steps.

August in Center City was hot, as close to unbearable as I ever wanted to get. Early in the morning the heat was already energy-sapping. Sulfur-tinged air from the oil refinery a mile down the Schuylkill River blanketed this end of town when there was no wind. I sat on the stoop and watched Linda play with the girl next door. Seth sat in the stroller next to me slobbering a piece of zwieback into submission.

Max walked up and down the steps of the three houses on my right. Each time he got to the bottom step of the third house he turned to see if I was watching. I was momentarily distracted and looked away. He took off running. He was fast but I was faster. I ran, scooped him up and planted his wriggling body on my hip. I was frustrated and sweating from the exertion.

I had planned to take them up to Fitler Square. At least there I got to talk to adults. Now I was stuck in my hot, airless house with three cranky children. Thank God I hadn't said I planned to go to the Square. With Max, I made an effort to resist making promises I might not be able to keep if he didn't behave. He remembered every promise I made and gave me a hard time if we didn't end up doing exactly what I had said we would do. I tried to make it clear we were staying home because he misbehaved but he never took responsibility for the consequences of his own bad behavior. He couldn't comprehend the logic of other people's rules. I sometimes felt as if we spoke two different languages. We used the same words but they clearly didn't have the same meanings.

I couldn't figure out why he didn't give up with the abortive running away. Each time he pulled this stunt, everyone ended up mad at him. Why couldn't he learn he couldn't escape, give up and enjoy what he *was* allowed to do? I took all three kids inside. Max protested and Linda shrieked with understandable fury. I don't think Seth really cared but he yelled in sympathy with Linda. She stormed upstairs. I put Seth in his playpen and set the bolts I had installed at the tops of the two outside doors. So far, I had always managed to unlock these before Pete got home but each time I set the bolts, the tension in my chest ratcheted up a few notches. Trying to balance Max's need to escape with his father's equally strong insistence on unlocked doors left me feeling like a rubber band stretched to the snapping point.

Beside myself with frustration that my day was once again shaped by Max's actions, I railed at him but stopped abruptly. Why did I bother? Nothing I said changed his behavior. I got the impression I baffled him with my dumb rules.

I listened for furniture being moved each time I went down to the basement to put another load of clothes into the washing machine. There was a pattern to the sounds. First the worn red table that had been mine as a child was pulled across the living room floor and pushed against the front door. Then one of the heavy plywood cubes that my father had made was dragged and hoisted onto the table. Heavy, it made a distinctive clunk. When I heard footsteps following this noise, I went up to the living room and put everything back. When I appeared, Max dropped the small rocker he was carrying to complete his ladder to freedom. He looked angry but he never protested and he never stopped trying. I wished I could figure out what was going on inside his head. This day, I got all the laundry sorted and folded, even the white wash with its plethora of small white articles of clothing. There were only four orphan socks—a record of sorts. A twinge of hope struggled to root itself in my consciousness. Maybe Max had bowed to the reality of following rules.

The door knocker banged. I ran upstairs. Afraid it was Pete, my heart raced as I unbolted and opened the front door. It was worse. A uniformed policeman stood on the marble step holding Max's hand. The officer was wearing leather riding boots and jodhpur-like trousers. I glanced out at the street expecting a horse. No horse. A motorcycle with a side-car chugged at the curb in the space behind my car. The officer frowned at me. "You should keep an eye on your kids, lady. You're lucky your little boy knows where he lives."

I was young but he looked like he should have been in grade school. It's weird to have some kid call me "lady" and give me a hard time, uniform or no uniform. I curbed the impulse to make a crack about his missing horse and said the next thing that crossed my mind. "I wish you hadn't brought him home in a motorcycle." The officer's frown deepened. He was wearing those curved sunglasses all the guys in the Air Force wore in pictures so I couldn't see his eyes. I blurted out my next thought. "Where was he this time?" I clearly shot to the top of his list of deadbeat moms.

"At the drugstore. What do you mean—this time?" The radio on the motorcycle squawked with a garbled call. He gave Max a sketchy pat on the head and said, "Take it easy, Sport. Gotta answer that call."

"Thank you for the ride, sir." The policeman walked around the sidecar, checked for oncoming traffic, threw his leg over the seat and roared off. Max watched with the starry-eyed look of a disciple beholding a long-hoped-for-miracle.

"He showed me his gun, Mom. But he wouldn't let me hold it." He looked up with a rapt expression, wanting me to share in his wonderful experience. "It's really big."

His innocent wonder made me sad. He looked up at me. "Were you worried?"

"Not yet but I would have been when I found out you were gone. I thought you were in Linda's room playing. How did you get out of the house? The doors were still locked."

He held out his hands. Two creosote splotched splinters stuck out of his right hand and a smaller one poked out of the ball of the left thumb.

"Where did those come from?"

"Linda's telephone pole. Can you take them out?"

What he called Linda's pole was in the next yard and a long way from the ground. It was still unbearably hot but dread made me shiver. "Show me how you got to the pole."

Linda glared at me when we went into her room then cringed and started to cry when she saw the horror on my face. Max had gotten out by going hand over hand along a thin guy wire supporting the phone line between the house and the pole. The end of the wire at the house was loosely attached to a small eyelet screwed into soft salmon brick. The line was easily sixteen feet above a brick-paved areaway.

I fought to keep from howling in concert with Linda. "You could have been killed."

I looked at him feeling helpless. He was a beautiful little boy. His eyes were large, utterly guileless and the same intense blue as his father's. He wouldn't be four years old for another three months. At times like this, I was torn between the instinctive need to save him from himself and the equally gripping wish to have a life where I got time off.

I shook my head and slumped against the wall wondering how I would get through the rest of that day, let alone the whole week. It was only ten-thirty and I already felt as though I had been carrying an enormous weight up an endless succession of hills stretching far beyond the horizon.

Max patted my leg. "It's okay, Mom. I knew I wouldn't fall. I wasn't afraid."

"I know. That's what scares me the most."

I sat with Linda. I knew she had suggested the guy wire as an escape route for Max. I couldn't blame her. He was a never-ending blight on her life. The trick was helping her understand I knew how she felt and that I empathized with her without saying anything negative about Max. It wasn't easy. Then I had to try to impress on her that helping Max escape from the house was *not* going to get rid of him permanently. If anything, it might injure him so badly he would take up even more of my time.

Linda and Max had nothing in common except their last name. Linda was an inherently social person. Pete had coined her "the rabble rouser." It was an apt name. If we had been able to go to Fitler Square, she would have been playing with other children now instead of sitting in her own room feeling helpless because Max refused to follow any rules. I did my best but her parting shot blew any sense I might have had that what I said made a difference. She looked at me through eyes narrowed to little more than slits and said, "Why is *Max* the only one you love? Why don't you care about Seth and me?"

Chapter 15

Nursery school was a godsend. I piled the three children into the car each morning after breakfast, took Max to school in West Philadelphia, drove back into Center City and across to Sansom Street then left Linda at kindergarten and had three hours with only Seth. He was a joy. He sang made-up songs as he played peacefully. A woman who adored him cleaned my house every Thursday. Life was definitely improving.

Pete flatly refused to go to the monthly meetings at Max's school. I felt naked each time I showed up alone at what were supposed to be meetings with both parents. The psychiatrist who presided over the initial screening was there sporadically. The social worker and psychologist usually ran the parent conferences. The first few times we met they spent a lot of time quizzing me on why Pete had chosen to avoid the discussions of Max's progress. It gradually dawned on them that I didn't know and their carping was making me feel defensive. The psychiatrist explained their concern. "We need to talk with the father on a regular basis. One of our most telling assessments is having the child act out family dynamics."

"How?"

"We have a doll house. We give the child small dolls to represent his or her family. We even make sure the dolls have the correct hair and eye and skin color. Max knew exactly what you and his siblings did all day. His big sister argued with him. His baby brother was carried around and took naps. You fixed cuts, cooked food, washed clothes and drove him to school. You never hit him. When you're angry, you stamp your feet and clap your hands. Is that right?"

"Yes. I know it sounds silly but it works. I also yell at him." I paused. "You didn't mention his father."

"No. That was the problem." He frowned and looked down at

the paper in front of him. "Max couldn't figure out what to do with the father doll. That in itself wasn't too far from the norm. Fathers are often gone during the child's waking hours. But Max appeared to be obsessed with the father doll."

"Obsessed how?"

"We asked him to imagine different times of day so we could get a sense of the family dynamics. He quickly positioned the rest of the family then shifted his father from place to place and became increasingly anxious because he couldn't decide what to do with him."

I nodded.

"That doesn't surprise you?"

"No. Pete hates being accountable to anyone. He'll walk out the door and disappear without saying where he's going or when he'll be back. Sometimes I don't even know he's gone. He could be gone for an hour or all day. A couple of times he was gone all night. This makes Max crazy."

"Crazy how?"

"Max wants absolutes. Pete's unpredictable. The first thing Max does each morning is check to see if Pete is still in bed. If he is Max watches him for a few minutes..."

"Just watches? He doesn't try to wake his father?"

I laughed. "No. Max seems to have figured out his father is not a morning person. I get the impression Max is just assuring himself Pete is there."

The social worker asked, "What does he do if Pete *isn't* in bed?"

"Asks me where he is. If I don't know, Max follows me around and keeps asking. Each time the phone rings he comes running and wants to know if it's Pete. Eventually he gets mad at me."

The psychiatrist frowned. "Why get mad at you?"

I had to think for a minute. "I get the impression he thinks I'm in charge of everyone in the family. I keep track of the kids—why don't I do a better job with their father? But it's probably just because I'm available."

The psychologist said, "How do *you* feel when your husband walks out and doesn't let you know where he's going?"

"Irritated—and insulted. I don't know why he does it so I read it from my perspective. I wouldn't walk off and leave him with the kids. I think it's thoughtless and rude."

"Have you told him how you feel?"

"Often. He just brushes me off."

"Does he understand it's hard on the children?"

"I've told him that too but he still does it."

"Why? Didn't he want children?"

Startled, I said, "*I* was the one who didn't want children. Pete wanted six kids."

"Why?"

I felt embarrassed. I wasn't comfortable stating assumptions that fringed on psychology. I was tempted to shrug and say I didn't know but this was something I had been thinking about recently. I looked down at my lap and mumbled, half hoping this would soften what I said. "I'm five years younger than Pete is. I think he mistook polite and even-tempered for soft and malleable. Any show of capability on my part scares him."

The social worker looked interested. "Has he said anything that makes you think this?"

"The other day he said 'Every time I think I've got you under control, you squirt out around the edges.'"

The men looked shocked. The social worker's mouth twisted into a smile. "An honest man. What triggered that?"

"I'd just replaced the washer on the kitchen faucet. It's no big deal. I'd seen my dad do it dozens of times. I thought Pete would be pleased."

The psychologist was frowning again. "How does this relate to the wish for six children?"

The social worker chuckled and said, "Six kids would keep her too busy to do anything on her own."

The psychiatrist frowned and said, "Are you saying he's a misogynist? Sorry, that means..."

I cut him off. "I know what it means. And, yes, I think he is although it hadn't occurred to me until my friend, Mary, commented on it."

He had the grace to look embarrassed at his assumption I wouldn't know the meaning of a technical term. "You think he wanted six children to keep you under his control?"

"Yes. Along with insisting we had to move the minute I got comfortable, made new friends and began having any sort of life separate from his. I guess that sounds egocentric. His need to move may have nothing to do with me. I may be confusing the end result with the reasoning behind his actions."

"What made you think it's a possibility?"

I told him about the timing of the move from Concord that lost me a semester's college credits.

"I can see why it occurred to you." He paused to write on something in a folder in his lap. When he looked up his eyes narrowed slightly as though he were trying to see me clearly. "Why *six* children?"

"His family life was pretty grim. He didn't get along with his brother or his mom and his father was away a lot of the time, and Pete once mentioned how lucky the six kids were in the family two doors away because there was always someone they could turn to for help when their parents turned weird and gave them a hard time."

Chapter 16

I had regular in-class meetings with Max's teachers. The school had interior courtyards so the children could have the benefit of outdoor air—sulfur fumes included—without escaping. I was in the courtyard one visiting day. Max was behind me stacking large wood squares. His teacher was describing his normal school day. Every few seconds she flicked her glance up, clearly a nervous tic. It was disconcerting. I fought the impulse to look around. I didn't want to embarrass her. One of the boys whined and yanked her skirt. "Why can't I do it?"

The teacher adopted a super-patient voice that verged on long-suffering. "Now, Josh. What did I tell you yesterday?"

"It's not fair. How come *he* gets to do it?"

"Because he proved he can do it without falling."

Feeling dread, I didn't want to turn around but I did. Max was going hand over hand along the gutter. He was already ten feet from the block ramp he had built to reach the gutter.

Josh shrieked with frustration, kicked the blocks into a heap and threw himself on the flagstones in a full-fledged tantrum.

Max looked at the scattered heap of blocks. For the first time he seemed to grasp that his swinging feet were a long way from the ground. He looked at me with mute appeal. I moved toward him. The teacher stopped me. "No, Max has to figure this out himself." She looked up. "Max, what did we do when Josh kicked over the blocks yesterday?"

"I jumped into the sand pile." He was cringing. He hated getting sand in his clothes.

The teacher nodded. "That's right. Go to the sand pile, curl up in a ball and drop. Remember to roll when you land."

I did my best to keep my face encouraging. I fervently hoped the teacher knew what she was doing. I also hoped their insurance would pay Max's hospital bill if he broke a limb. We were strapped just paying the tuition.

Josh stopped kicking and screaming, climbed up on the picnic table in the middle of the courtyard, unzipped his fly, pulled out his penis, announced he had to pee RIGHT NOW and did. The teacher looked at him. "Josh, we discussed this yesterday. You know where we empty our bladders. It isn't in the courtyard." She motioned to her assistant. "Molly, as soon as Josh is finished would you please take him to the lavatory so he can wash his hands?"

By the time the teacher turned back to Max, he was above the large sand pile in the corner. He stared down at it then looked at me hoping I would over-ride the teacher. It was hard but I said, "You can do it."

The teacher nodded with approval. "We're teaching him consequences. He has a problem with the concept."

The psychologist had said we should encourage Max to follow his own instincts and do our best to stop telling him he was wrong when he behaved in ways we couldn't predict. Every time Max went beyond the parameters we considered appropriate for his behavior, we were to acknowledge his right to make some of his own rules and back off unless what he was doing could cause him to get hurt or harm someone else. This may have worked in a controlled and finite school setting but was harder than it sounded out in the real world.

The concept drove my mother-in-law wild. She didn't have a permissive bone in her body. She was a strong believer in immediate harsh punishment. She told us we were ruining him. She may have been right but I hadn't noticed what we did or didn't do made much difference to Max. He liked approval, particularly from Pete but not enough to alter his behavior.

Being permissive with Max yet expecting the other kids to follow rules just made the other kids resent him even more. It might have had some benefit in the long run but seemed to increase the havoc in an already chaotic family. So we went back to doing our best to help Max follow the norms that would be expected in the real world. We weren't too successful.

The evening after the school visit where Max did his hand-over-hand along the drain and dropped into the sand box, I told Pete how I had spent my day. He looked at me with a disgusted expression. "That's what goes on in the *normal* nursery division? I guess we should be glad Max isn't in the 'sub-normal' or 'really whacked-out' nurseries."

I knew his comment wasn't politically correct but I couldn't help laughing.

Chapter 17

The agency where Pete worked had a client whose major product was ice cream. From April until September this account generated enough work to keep an artist working full-time. Each year the agency had to decide which artist would be pulled from his regular accounts to handle this. It was an unpopular assignment. The head art director for the ice cream account was the heavy-drinking man whose work I had finished at the dinner party in Levittown. After testing me with a few more freelance projects, he asked me if I could take on a large portion of the artwork for the ice cream account this year.

I was delighted. I lined up baby sitters I knew I could trust, enrolled Max in the day camp recommended by the nursery school and felt like a person with a past and a future.

My favorite part of the day was lunch. The idea that I could eat when and what I wanted was heady. No more peanut butter and jelly or toasted cheese and tomato soup lunches. I had a drawing board and phone line at the agency and my regular board at home.

Like Cinderella, I had a non-negotiable curfew. I left at three o'clock to collect Max at camp, took the baby sitter home and made dinner. The first week or so this made the art directors uneasy but I always took home any pending jobs and had them done and delivered the first thing in the morning, so they relaxed.

The first time I spent the night cradling the head of a child with stomach flu, it took all my will to go through my normal morning routine, dress properly and show up at the agency without commenting on my all-nighter-with-sick-kid exhaustion.

When I first started working, Pete had said, "Don't ever discuss your problems with the kids at work. You're suspect already because you're a woman with a family working in a man's job. No matter what goes on at home, show up with a smile on your face and a positive attitude. That's what men do."

That turned out to be wise advice. Any time I complained to Pete about being overwhelmed, he shrugged and said, "You don't have to work." I knew he was right. I was the one going against the norms of the time.

I should have spent more time figuring out the significance of his insistence that he was the only one who *had* to work outside the home. But I didn't. I just worked harder and took pride in the fact that I made it look easy. 1958 was not a time when women won points for working outside the home unless they were widowed. The sad thing about the era was that the women were their own worst enemies. I was fortunate I worked in a field where there were more or less set prices for different jobs no matter who did them. Salaried women fared far worse even if they were the only provider for the family. Gender discrimination was a fact of life. In the late fifties the ceiling holding women 'in their place' was made of government-approved cast iron.

The need to please had been beaten into my marrow from the moment the doctor grabbed my heels, lifted me up as far as the umbilical cord would stretch and said, "You have a little girl." Even when I was so tired I had to concentrate so I didn't walk into walls, I felt compelled to cook the way I always had to prove I wasn't neglecting my family. A well-cooked meal was the only accomplishment Pete ever praised. This spurred my efforts. No take-out or pre-packaged food in *my* house. My macaroni and cheese began with an impeccably smooth white sauce. We had pies and puddings I made from scratch for dessert: the puddings were topped with custard sauce or real whipped cream, the pies with ice cream.

I knew this was a failing on my part. Why did I need to make the point over and over that I hadn't lowered my standards just because I was working long hours?

I had never heard the term *super mom*. I don't think it had been invented in the late 1950s. I sometimes wonder now if I would have needed to keep proving I was very good at all the expected womanly attributes if Max had been just another normal little boy instead of an off-the-wall child who was noticed, criticized and automatically assumed to be raised by an uncaring, incompetent mother. In the time period stretching from 1950 to well into the 1980s, fathers weren't factored into the blame equation for difficult children unless they were gutter-draping drunks or child beaters. Every psychologist's diagnosis from profound autism to schizophrenia was blamed on the mother's alleged coldness and secret lack of love for her children. It was this 'secret' bit that got mothers coming and going. A woman could appear to be the most instinctively warm, maternal person imaginable and still qualify as a 'refrigerator mom' because some man with a doctorate in psychology or psychiatry had decided mothers were the root of all mental aberrations.

Pete counted on my need to be an impressive cook. He often brought the men in his group home for supper when they had to work late. The men were funny and appreciative. I enjoyed the meals but found the clean-up daunting when I had to wash dishes and ready the kitchen for breakfast before I could even start the hours of work waiting on my drawing board. No one ever offered to help. Pete was a charismatic alpha male and this was his home turf. Any man who felt awkward about leaving me with a mess was intimidated by Pete's implied message that men in *his* house didn't do dishes.

Some ornery part of my mind knew the whole terrific cook routine was feeding into an agenda Pete had in mind. I began small rebellions. One evening after putting in a day working at the agency, I cooked and served Pete and two men from the office a crab and fresh mushroom quiche and steamed new asparagus with hollandaise sauce. When I had cleared the plates and poured coffee for everyone, I brought out a still warm lemon pudding cake then sat down and put my napkin back in my lap.

Pete looked at me with the bereft expression of a little boy who had just discovered his Christmas present was mittens his mom had made and said, "Didn't you make poured custard?"

I looked at him and wondered what was going through his mind. Not wanting to embarrass the two guests, I just said, "No. I never make it with lemon pudding cake. There's heavy cream in the fridge if you want." I started eating my pudding.

He frowned and said, "I *would* like cream, if that's all you have."

Knowing he expected me to get up and get the cream, I said, "It's behind the milk." And took another bite of pudding. He never did get the cream. But we all paid for my brief rebellion.

He and the two men went back to the office. I was asleep on the couch when he came home. He didn't answer when I said, "Hi." The next morning he was still not speaking to me. I just hoped he would get out of the house without lashing out at the kids. Max was down in the basement watching TV by the time I dragged myself downstairs. He liked to watch Sunrise Semester. I figured as long as he wasn't watching horror movies, I had no objection to morning TV. He seemed to have lost interest in escaping now that he had an outlet in nursery school and camp but I didn't push my luck. I didn't unlock the doors until I heard Pete getting out of the shower.

We had only one bathroom so I always showered, dressed and had breakfast ready by the time Pete appeared. Morning wasn't his best time of day so I rarely said anything.

Since I had to pick up the baby sitter and take Max to camp, Pete always left before I did and walked or took the bus. His feet appeared at the top of the open stairwell dividing the living and dining rooms. Freshly showered and shaved, he walked down to the first floor with a measured step. The scent of bay rum followed him into the kitchen. Damn! He was a great-looking man. I would have loved to stroke his smooth cheek but I checked my impulse. Even if he weren't feeling crabby this morning, he hated affectionate moves unless they were a precursor to sex.

I handed him the cup of black coffee I'd poured when I first heard his step on the stairs. He took it without acknowledging me then grabbed the plate with his freshly buttered English muffin still hot from the toaster.

Max said, "Dad, the sun makes corphil in leaves. This gives trees energy."

Pete's face twisted into a sneer. "Where the hell did you get *that* piece of misinformation?"

Max's face still had the wonder of an explorer who had just found treasure. I realized he hadn't picked up on Pete's contempt yet but he would before Pete got through with him. "The man on TV said that."

Max's innocence made him too vulnerable. I had told Pete his criticism made Max feel devastated. The poor kid was only four years old. Why couldn't Pete give him the credit he deserved? But Pete couldn't seem to help himself. "Stop saying stupid things. You don't know what you're talking about. Corphil, for Christ's sake. If you're going to spout shit you don't know anything about at least learn to say it right. It's chlorophyll, not corphil."

Coming from Pete's mouth corphil sounded like a four-letter word. A stunned look crossed Max's face.

I tried to distract Pete. "Do you want more coffee?" He put the half-full cup of coffee on the top of the brick wall separating the kitchen from the dining room and walked out without replying. As usual, he bent and nuzzled Seth before he left.

I automatically went through the normal early morning routine all the while wondering why I had married a man with such a mean streak. I drove Max out to camp on auto-pilot while I tried to decide if I even realized before we were married that he had this capacity to deliberately hurt people.

Everyone had the capacity to lash out if provoked beyond some set point but they usually recognized they had gone over a line, felt guilty and tried to make amends. Pete seemed to be unaware of the consequences of his nastiness. Or was this assumption of his innocence just my attempt to excuse his behavior?

I eventually had to face the fact that I *had* seen his cruel sarcastic side before we were married. But it was always directed at me. And for some reason I made the choice to see the wit, not the cruelty. Directed at my child, I saw only the cruelty.

Chapter 18

Pete had always dreamed of owning a sailboat. A man he worked with grew up around boats, loved sailing and nurtured the same dream. The two men joined forces and bought a Comet, a sixteen-foot racing sloop with a movable centerboard. It was a sleek boat easily sailed by two people. Pete insisted it was something the whole family would enjoy. He and the friend hauled the boat to a mooring on the bay side of Long Beach Island on the New Jersey shore. Because it was a small racing sloop that would be affected by even a minor number of barnacles, the boat had to be dropped into the water and hauled back out and hosed off each time it was taken out in the saltwater bay. It had a shallow draft when the centerboard was up but still drew enough water so it could only be launched and pulled out of the water at high tide. When it wasn't in use, it sat on a trailer in a boat parking lot with a tarp lashed around it.

High tide came at ridiculous hours of the day and night. I got sea-sick on a porch swing unless I was the one pushing it so I was not dying to go sailing. And the kids were too young to have any interest. They did love the beach but even this wore thin fast when one of the kids needed a lavatory and nothing on the island was open. There weren't even thickets of bushes that were not in someone's yard.

When it was warm enough to get out of the car, Seth dug in the sand. Max threw horseshoe crabs back into the bay the poor creatures had just spent hours wriggling out of and Linda and I stared at each other in bored frustration.

It took me a lot of middle-of-the-night-trips to Long Beach Island nestled in the back seat of the Beetle with three sleeping children to convince Pete I was not being a spoilsport when I pointed out Comets were not family-friendly day sailors. I finally made him understand it was okay to go sailing without the family in tow. I could see I was blasting another dream he had nurtured. He had one last try at making the boat a family affair and shanghaied Max into going sailing. Max was thrilled. For once he didn't have to compete for Pete's attention. The man who co-owned the boat thought Max was delightful. It looked as though it would be a perfect day for everyone.

One of the well-known aspects of the bay between Long Beach Island and the mainland was the freaky aspect of wind directions. These changed frequently without warning or logic. The two men launched the boat without any problem and sailed back and forth for a few hours. Then one of the area's freak storms blew up. Because the tide had dropped by this point the water at the ramp was too shallow to get the boat out of the water. Comets were sensitive boats. This was part of the reason they were fun to sail but they were no good in high seas. The two men lashed Max to the mast and spent the next few hours desperately trying not to get swamped and sink. Max was thrown from side to side and understandably certain the boat was about to sink. He shrieked in a high thin wail because he couldn't make these two dumb men understand this very obvious fact. Lashed to the mast he couldn't jump overboard and swim to shore. He was way on the far side of abject terror. Tacking desperately and using every bit of skill they possessed, the two men finally sailed the boat through the narrow slip before the next high tide had run back out. They untied Max, hauled the boat out of the water, washed it and battened it down. Too exhausted to sluice themselves off, they arrived at the house an hour and a half later still coated with rime. White and stiffened by hours of salt spray, every hair stood out. They looked like the old men with bristling eyebrows who frequented the Irish bar on the corner.

Max was still shaking.

Chapter 19

Max loved watching *Lassie* on TV. Like most kids then, he decided he wanted a dog exactly like the beautiful Collie featured in the show. I talked it over with Pete and he agreed it might be a good idea. A friend with a nice dog suggested I go to the pound. She said they had some dogs that were already neutered and had all their shots.

There were a couple of puppies at the pound that looked as though they had Collie blood but Max had settled on a dog who was obviously a full-grown white miniature poodle. She was an appealing little dog with bright button eyes and a cheerful expression but as far from the TV Lassie as possible.

"Max, this dog is full-grown. Its fur will always be white and curly and it isn't going to get any larger."

"Yes it will. It's going to get big and look just like Lassie."

"Max, you have to believe me, this dog is *not* going to grow bigger and this is the way it will always look." Nothing I said swayed him. Only five, he didn't understand the implacable constants of heredity. This was the dog he wanted. He said he would call it Lassie.

The attendant said, "You could do worse. She's house-trained, spayed, has had all her shots, eats much less than a collie, doesn't shed hair and will be happy to use your backyard to run around in and do her business."

The dog sounded like a pet-owner's dream. That was when I should have asked why the dog's former owners were getting rid of her if she was such a gem. We soon found out. Lassie was a selective nipper. She never broke the skin; she just lunged and triggered an instinctive flinch away from her sharp teeth. She preferred male ankles. The first time she tried nipping Pete, he lifted her with the side of his foot and sailed her across the room. She picked herself up and shook her head. After that she often rested her head on her paws and stared at him with an intense, unsettling gaze. I had the feeling she was plotting something but she was smart enough to leave Pete's ankles alone.

Max tried to teach her to do some of the clever things the TV Lassie did. Nothing seemed to work but he kept at it. He repeatedly asked me when the dog was going to start looking like the real Lassie. Each time he asked, I explained this would never happen but he just ignored me and persisted in his belief she would get larger, develop a long pointed nose, red silky hair, a long sweeping tail and know how to do Lassie tricks. On the TV show the Collie's tricks always centered on saving Timmy, the little boy in the series.

I knew this was why Max wanted a dog exactly like the one on the show. I was cheered that he seemed to understand he needed constant saving. What he hadn't grasped was the fact that Timmy's perils came from the outside world. Max's were no less threatening but came from his own actions and misperceptions of the world. I worried about his reaction when he finally understood wanting something as drastic as changing a poodle into a collie would have no influence on the outcome. This seemed like a crucial lesson. I assumed Max would figure it out eventually but I had no idea how he would react when his dream of a loving dog that would protect him from harm fizzled.

Lassie would chase a ball and bring it back but even when Max explained exactly how to do it, she didn't develop any skill at unlocking and pushing open windows the way the TV Lassie did when the house was on fire. His dog just continued to do what she did best. She nipped boys' ankles. After a while she concentrated on Seth's ankles because it made him furious and got a satisfying response. Seth was two and said very little but what he did say was clear. Every time the dog became bored, she made a run at Seth's ankles. Lassie was much faster than Seth was. He tried kicking her but this just delighted the dog and presented her sharp teeth with a great target. So he grabbed the broom and tried whacking her with it. He shrieked, "Damn dog, damn dog, damn dog," and swung the broom like a club but Lassie moved too fast to hit. Attacking Seth became her favorite game.

A childless older couple lived down the street from us. They thought Lassie was 'simply adorable'. They were so taken with her they often borrowed her so they could take her on walks.

Lassie finally figured out how to get back at Pete for his summary rejection via foot-assisted air lift: she left a pile of dog feces on the exact center of his pillow.

Max was so grossed out when I showed him Lassie's not too subtle message to Pete, he seemed relieved when I said we had to give the dog away. He knew the *real* Lassie would *never* befoul Pete's pillow. Any worthwhile dog would be smart enough not to challenge his father.

I spoke to the older couple. They were delighted to take the dog. They were serious dog-lovers. They thought it was funny when Lassie ate the man's Stetson hat. It was a perfect match. They renamed the dog Louis the Fourteenth and called her Teeny. Max never mentioned Lassie again.

Chapter 20

The nursery school program ended with pre-kindergarten. At my last meeting with the psychologist and social worker they told me Max wouldn't do well in public school. We had an excellent one in this part of downtown Philadelphia but the classes were large and kindergarten was just a half day. They insisted he would do better in a private school where the classes were small, less rigid and ran from nine to three. A school in Center City came well-recommended and I liked the people I met when I visited there.

It was closer than the nursery school and the schedule allowed me to combine Max and Linda's drop offs and pick-ups. Max liked kindergarten. The teacher was smart and had enough imagination to treat each child as an individual. She found Max fascinating and he responded well to her encouragement. At our parent/teacher meeting, she noted that he hadn't bonded with any of the other children but she didn't see this as a problem.

"He's a loner. Not unusual with really bright kids. He has a great vocabulary, likes the sound of words. He's a nice boy, doesn't throw his weight around."

I nodded. "That's good as long as he doesn't allow himself to be bullied."

"True. I only mention it because super-bright children can be mean to children who are slower to grasp new things. The only problem I ever have is his wandering off. When we visited the battleship at the Philadelphia Navy Yard last week he gave us a real scare."

Apprehensive, I frowned. "He said something about visiting the captain. He was so off-hand about it, I just assumed it was part of the tour."

The teacher laughed. "No way. We weren't supposed to see anyone but their public relations guy.

"How did he end up with the captain? Was it really the captain?"

"Oh, yeah. The real one. One minute Max was standing with the other kids watching the officer describe how they batten down the deck in high seas. Then he was gone."

"How did you finally find him?"

"The PR guy made an announcement that a small boy was loose and asked anyone who knew where he was to let him know. Boy did he snap to attention when the captain called him back. Max was up on the bridge. The captain said he would make sure Max got back safely but he was showing him some of the equipment on the bridge so it might be a few minutes."

Now I knew why Max was beaming in the official picture of the outing.

Chapter 21

Downtown Philadelphia was a good place to live. There were always places to go and things to do. Linda and I liked to take the bus down to John Wanamaker's store on Market Street, catty-cornered from the City Hall. We made a ritual of shopping even if the only thing she needed was socks. We then took the elevator up to the Crystal room for lunch. The waitresses were kind and didn't rush us. They understood little girls who went shopping with their mothers.

Before Linda knew how to read she liked me to tell her what was on the menu and describe each item in detail. After this part of the ritual was satisfied, she always got the tea sandwiches with the tiny cup of soup in the center of the plate. I think it was a visual thing with her. At home we ate crusts. At Wanamaker's, not only were there no crusts but the four sandwiches were all diamond shaped with different breads and fillings. She finished every sandwich and never commented on the fillings even when they were ones she would never eat at home. We finished with hot fudge sundaes.

Max and I went to the Franklin institute and the Art Museum. He spent most of the time there in the area with the armor and weapons. The suits of armor were all much smaller than any current adult male I knew. This fascinated Max. One of the full suits would have fit him and he was much smaller than most boys his age. He wanted me to explain who would have worn it.

"Did they let boys my age fight in wars?"

"Maybe. No one knows."

"Yeah but could they fight if they wanted to?"

"I wouldn't think so. People were supposedly smaller then. The boy who wore this could have been nine or ten."

A man listening to us talk volunteered that he had read the small suits were samples the armorers made to show how good their work was. Max just rolled his eyes. He preferred the idea of small boys clanking around in shiny armor.

He turned his back on the man, stood in front of the weapons case and mimicked how fierce *he* would have been if he were given a hefty sword or a mace with barbs all over its surface. He looked like he could do a lot of damage for a skinny little kid. And enjoy every minute of it. Suddenly feeling chilled, I clutched my elbows. Maybe six-year-olds *were* used as soldiers.

When we went to The Franklin Institute it was so full of Max-type exhibits my only problem was getting him to leave. I read every explanation posted with the individual parts of the exhibits. Max was like a spring-loaded toy figure. He leaped from section to section the moment I got to the end of the written placards. He seemed to be reading them along with me. The only problem I had with the Franklin Institute was the questions he peppered me with in subsequent weeks. He remembered virtually everything I had read to him. I didn't. I grasped the overall logic but didn't always retain the details. He did.

An older couple with no children of their own and a lot of patience lived directly across Pine Street. They found Max fascinating and often invited him to go places with them. He thrived on the undivided attention of two approving adults. One day they decided to take him to a polo match. Max wore chinos and a polo shirt. I explained the shirt was named for the match he was going to see. He wanted to know why. I had never been to a polo match so I told him I assumed the players wore polo shirts.

His experience with horses was limited to Roy Rogers and Gene Autry movie re-runs and Lone Ranger episodes on TV. Fortunately, the couple who took him had a sense of humor. Max spent the entire match trying to figure out what the men riding the horses had done with their guns. At one point the man who took him had to grab the collar of his shirt and hold on to him when Max started out onto the playing field. Max was sure he would be able to see the guns if he got closer to the horses.

Pete took Max to the museum at the University of Pennsylvania just across the Schuylkill River from our house. They both looked a little frazzled by the time they got home but they did it again so they must have enjoyed the outing.

One weekend afternoon, Pete asked Max if he wanted to go to his office. Max was thrilled and the two of them drove off. Plagued by a mental image of Max loose in the middle of the art department with its paints, matte knives and partially finished artwork on drawing boards kept me literally breathless. I only realized I was forgetting to breathe when I took an involuntary gasp. I tried to will myself to fill my lungs normally but it's hard to override gut-level anxiety. I gasped the afternoon away.

When I heard the unmistakable sound of the VW beetle parking in front of the house, I ran to the window and peeked out. Pete looked concerned but they were still talking and Max was glowing. He clutched a handful of layout paper with drawings all over the pages. I must have looked panicked when I realized some of the pages were partially finished layouts and asked Max where they came from. I had visions of being up all night trying to re-do the work and sneak them onto the respective artists' drawing boards in the early morning.

"This is stuff I found in the trash room. Dad said I wasn't allowed to go into any of the little rooms where the desks were but he didn't say anything about the trash room so I played there."

"What trash room?"

"It's a door around the back by the freight elevator."

When I asked how the day went, Pete just shrugged and said, "I know a lot more about where stuff is kept on the floor now."

When he came home the following day, Pete handed me a notice that had been circulated in the art department. It asked artists to leave small children at home because of danger to equipment, personal belongings and the child or children.

I looked up at Pete. "What equipment?"

"The Lucy was down all morning. It had been cranked too far." (Before the advent of computers, the Camera Lucida, always referred to as Lucy, was used to scale artwork up or down. It was in constant use because no writer, artist, or account executive thought he had earned his keep unless he made changes.)

"What personal belongings?"

"Fred's stash of Clark bars and Art's jar of licorice sticks. Max left two sticks."

I looked around to make sure Max hadn't gotten out of bed. "Do they know Max created the havoc?"

"No. A lot of people were signed in during the morning. A few had kids with them so it was just a general notice."

Pete and I had a busy social life and took advantage of the city itself. Many of the plays and musicals getting ready for New York tried out in Philadelphia. We saw them all. The orchestra was top-notch and ballet companies from all over the world came to town. Life was as good as it could get. Until Pete was asked to move to Chicago.

His title was Art Director. He functioned in that role and had developed an incredible talent for turning out beautifully executed drawings that conveyed movement and expression and made a series of flat drawings come to life. Referred to as comps if these were for print ads, or story-boards if for TV, these drawings showed clients what proposed commercials or other advertising would look like. He had been traveling frequently in the last year, had spent considerable time in Detroit working on a major account there and in Chicago on an equally large account. Earlier, he had been asked to move to Detroit. He refused this move without a moment's pause. Because of his talent for capturing the sense of the planned presentation and his ability to work long hours, no matter where he lived, he was going to spend much of his time at the agency's other offices every time they were getting ready for major presentations. He could have refused the Chicago move but he didn't.

I recognized the signs. He was getting restless and wanted a change. We had been married for nine years and we'd moved six times. I knew moving would be a major mistake. The family was stable. I had work I enjoyed and was well paid for it. I loved where we lived and the city itself. Max was happy in the kindergarten at his school. Linda was in an excellent school full of fascinating people.

I tried to get Pete to talk about the impact his move would have on the family as a whole. He said he was too busy to waste time discussing it.

I talked with the psychologist at Max's old nursery school. He set up a joint conference with the psychiatrist who oversaw Max's case and the social worker. This time Pete did go to the meeting. The three experts made a compelling case for staying in Philadelphia. They told us moving Max at this point would have a damaging effect on his progress.

I nodded. "He hates change. He seems to need every day to be the same even when he doesn't like what's going on around him." Pete's eyes turned opaque. He heard what each of us said but was obviously not interested in anyone else's point of view.

He wouldn't have been fired if we stayed here; he was just bored. I told him I wouldn't move. He took the transfer anyway, lived in a hotel in downtown Chicago and came to Philadelphia a couple times a month if he could. I got the impression he liked the arrangement. The hotel washed and cleaned his clothes and he could decide where and what he would eat. He could hang out in bars as late as he wanted. He saw all the current movies and read the papers over a leisurely breakfast without interruptions from a wife and children. He called most days, asked what was going on and filled me in on office politics. He was entertaining over a phone line. Pete's visits were brief and chaotic. We usually entertained or went out to parties. He made an effort to be charming. He was a break in the routine. Fun to have around for a couple of days but by Sunday afternoon his sarcastic side started to pop to the surface and I realized I was becoming tense waiting for one of his cutting barbs. I knew I would miss him at times but was relieved each time he left. I had the sense we all were, even Max. The minute Pete disappeared inside the airport terminal, the tension level in the car dropped noticeably. With him in Chicago, I didn't have to camp on the couch and fight to stay awake until he came home. I could lock and bolt the doors and go to bed when I wanted.

Life was dull but I had nothing against dull if it was easier. And it was. The kids thought macaroni and cheese tasted great with a cream of mushroom soup base. Their favorite vegetable was the green bean casserole topped with those crispy tinned onions from the recipe on the onion can. They even liked frozen fish sticks if I made plenty of tarter sauce full of chopped dill pickles and no onions. And even when Pete was in Chicago, the rest of us were invited to family parties.

Chapter 22

Pete was living in Chicago in September of 1959 when Max started first grade. His school had two first grade teachers: a skilled, well-trained one who had asked if Max could be in her classroom and a sweet young woman with an English degree from a good school who had no teacher training whatsoever. He got the untrained one.

His first report card had only the caustic comment that Max could read *The New York Times* from cover to cover *in spite of* the fact that he didn't want to do the exercises with the rest of the class. When I asked the teacher what the exercises were, she indicated yellow lined pages with CAT, HAT and every other possible three-letter word ending with AT taped to the top of the blackboard. When I asked her if he was disruptive or disobedient, she was defensive. "He's quiet but just wants to read books instead of writing out the exercises the other children have to do."

"That's bad?"

She had the grace to blush. "The other children get upset because he doesn't have to sit at his desk. You really shouldn't have taught him how to read."

"I didn't. He taught himself." She obviously didn't believe me.

A week later, I found folded wads of newspaper in his pants pocket when I was sorting clothes for the washer. I asked him if I should keep them.

"No, I read them already."

I looked at one. "How come you're reading the want ads?"

"It's all I could find to read when I was out in the hall. It was in the trash."

He was offhand about it. He said his teacher sent him out to the hall because he didn't like to sit at his desk while the kids wrote out exercises. "She won't let me take a book with me so I read stuff I find in the wastebasket."

I asked his teacher why she was doing this. "That's what we do here for punishment. Most kids hate it. Max doesn't seem to care." She shook her head. "I told him the next time he wouldn't sit at his desk and write out words, I would send him down to the headmaster's office. I understand that *really* makes them behave." Totally unaware this was supposed to be avoided at any cost, Max loved it. He could hardly wait to tell me how much fun he had with the headmaster. "He let me staple things."

I made another attempt to persuade Max's teacher to consider a more positive way to work with him. "He can sit for hours if he has a book to read or a challenging puzzle to solve."

"That's not possible. He has to sit at his desk and print the words along with the other children. That's the way I'm supposed to teach the children to read."

I knew two of the boys in the class. Both were bullies. One was twice Max's size. Even with me in the classroom, the larger of the two boys couldn't resist giving Max a shove that almost knocked him off his feet. The teacher flinched but didn't reprimand the boy. *He* was the one who should have been sitting in the hall but the teacher was clearly afraid of him. Or she had been told to give him special attention because his parents or grandparents were big contributors.

I spoke with the experienced teacher. She said, "I tried to have him transferred to my room but they won't do it. That would give me fifteen children and leave his teacher with only twelve. I feel so frustrated every time I see him sitting in the hall. It's such a pointless waste to punish him for being so smart. It not only gives him all the wrong messages, he doesn't even know it's a punishment."

"Would moving him to a higher grade solve anything?"

"Not in his case. If he were large and mature for his age, maybe but he's the smallest kid even in first grade. He's such a

98

nice child but painfully naive. He'd be the target of every bully in the class with an older, even larger bunch of children because he can't figure out the rules well enough to protect himself."

Around this time his pediatrician prescribed a low dose of Rauwolfia, a centuries-old herbal medicine used in India to cure mental illness and snakebites. It was supposed to help calm anxiety. I wasn't sure what it did for snakebites. If I had been attacked by a cobra, anxiety would have been the least of my worries. We stopped it by mutual agreement because Max didn't like the way it made him feel. His doctor and I agreed his difficulty with first grade wasn't the result of anxiety.

That spring, the headmaster asked to meet with me. He looked at me then down at his hand. Clearly embarrassed, he was flipping a letter opener back and forth. "Max won't be asked to enroll in second grade."

I felt as though the bottom had just dropped out of my lungs but kept my face impassive. "Why not? He likes it here."

He met my eyes, seemingly relieved at my matter-of-fact tone. I wondered how many mothers burst into tears when they were told their child was being banished from the school. "Max is a delightful, incredibly intelligent boy but he doesn't get it."

"Get it? Is he a discipline problem?"

"Not in the classic sense. He doesn't defy the rules. He doesn't even know they exist."

I nodded. A familiar weight settled on my chest. I felt trapped.

The headmaster continued. "Let me give you an example of the problem we're dealing with now. Max's teacher was concerned because he won't do the exercises along with the rest of the class."

"He already *knows* how to read. What will he gain by printing simple words he could read when he was three?"

"Nothing. But the rest of the children would benefit. As it is now, he disrupts the class because the other students spend the time they should be learning to read fussing because he gets away with not doing the exercises."

"So the teacher sends Max out to the hall." It was easy to see suggesting the teacher was incompetent would be a waste of my time but I was sorely tempted.

"Yes. Only Max didn't understand that this was a bad thing."

"No. He likes it there. He can read the want ads in peace." I tried to keep the bitterness I felt out of my voice.

The headmaster looked startled. He had an expressive face. I could see he wanted to know why I made the acid comment about want ads but apparently decided it might lead to areas he didn't want to discuss.

He finally nodded. "Right. So his teacher sent him to my office. The other children would have been horrified. Max walked into my office with a delighted smile, greeted me and shook my hand. He does have beautiful manners...we don't see much of that these days. And he asked me what he could do to help."

"I understand you let him staple pages together. He enjoyed that."

"Yes. And he opened the stapler to check if it needed staples then asked me where the staples were so he could fill it. Made me felt incompetent. I've never figured out how to open the thing. I just give it to my secretary and ask her to fill it."

I laughed. "I know how you feel."

He frowned then lifted his shoulders in a brief shrug. "His teacher sent him to my office every day last week. I finally told Max if I saw him in my office one more time, I would have to send him home. I knew we were in trouble when his face lit up and he said, 'In a school bus?'"

Chapter 23

Pete finally told me he was staying in Chicago. If I wanted to move fine, otherwise I was on my own. He wasn't going to live in Philadelphia.

He had been living in a hotel in downtown Chicago at the agency's expense; the normal procedure until a transferee was able to resettle his family. Someone from billing obviously complained about the hotel bill Pete was running up because I refused to move. The complaint worked its way down to the head of the art department. On the rare occasions when I saw the head art director, it was clear he had no idea who I was. He acted as though I were just another nameless company employee of some sort. It was a very large agency.

I don't know who told him Pete's wife was the freelance artist who had handled the ice cream account for the last two summers but someone clearly did. I had been doing work for different art directors off and on all through the winter but had not yet started work on that summer's stint on the ice cream account. The head art director stopped me one day shortly after Pete gave me his ultimatum, called me in to his office and told me the company wanted me to go to Chicago. That's what the agency expected from wives. He added that the agency could replace me as an artist but not as Pete's wife. He had already assigned the ice cream account to someone else and wouldn't feel comfortable giving me any other artwork under the circumstances.

He mentioned there had always been concern about having two members of the family working for the agency. I knew this was true. They did have an anti-nepotism policy. When they considered me important to them as an artist, they had gotten around this by having me bill in my maiden name. Now that I had become more important as a wife, they didn't feel comfortable hiding my identity.

This was all couched in smooth logic. I was a good, dependable artist but according to Pete, a perfect wife. Pete on the other hand was an artist who would be impossible to replace. He didn't ask me how Pete scored as a husband. The head art director was a good salesman and felt comfortable with what he was doing. His attitude was the norm in March of 1960.

I was so appalled that it took a few seconds for the full import of what he had said to sink in. I stared at him, trying to sort out my feelings. Did the man even realize I was a separate person? Something more than Pete's wife? I was suddenly so furious that all I could do was stand up, nod and walk out. I couldn't even manage a smile. People spoke to me as I walked to the elevator but I didn't answer; I was afraid if I opened my mouth I would start screaming and not be able to stop. By the time the elevator reached the lobby, my initial fury had turned to desolation. There were no anti-discrimination laws at that time. Wives would probably have been excluded if there were.

I had been naive to believe that I was finally established as an artist in my own right. I was wrong but that was my second mistake. My first one was gambling with a man I didn't understand.

From what little I was able to glean from Pete's mother, Pete's father had insisted on frequent, arbitrary moves but when she discovered she was pregnant with her first son, she flatly refused to move again. And they never did. Pete insisted I was a perfect wife but obviously not as perfect as his mother had been.

The next morning, I was standing in our backyard watching Linda playing with the little girl who lived behind us. Seth stood next to them, one hand propped on his hip. He nodded his head occasionally. He had been diagnosed with alternating esotropia, a form of lazy eye and wore horn-rimmed glasses with tape over the lens on his dominant eye so he always looked studious. I couldn't decide if he was taking mental notes on the complicated game the girls were constructing with lined-up popsicle sticks and small gray stones or keeping time to a song in his head. Max was in his room reading.

The house cast an oblique shadow across the sixteen-foot-wide yard. Exhausted from a sleepless night spent worrying about what I could do to survive if I stayed in Philadelphia, it took me a few seconds to realize the shadow of the roof peak had something moving on it. A second later what was clearly a small shadow head reared up and looked into the backyard. Max. I knew he was comfortable three stories above the ground. He didn't seem to have any grasp of the damage a small body would suffer falling off a roof ridge so high off the ground. I was terrified but couldn't let him know how frightened I was. I didn't dare look around. I willed my voice to be calm and mean at the same time. "Max, get back into the bathroom, NOW!"

Linda looked up. I hoped she was at the wrong angle to see his shadow but decided I had better distract her. She would shriek if she saw him. Her shrieks could dislodge a lurking buzzard.

So I asked her a question. "Have you decided how to play the game?" She went into an involved set of instructions. It turned out they had made up the rules before they did anything else. She liked to plan ahead.

I watched the shadow lump on the roof ridge. It stopped, turned around and started back to the bathroom window. I tried to nod at appropriate intervals in Linda's explanation but was so frightened I could tell I was blowing it.

"Mom, you're not listening. Why did you ask me if you don't even care?"

"Sorry, I was just distracted." It was chilly but I could feel sweat prickling my scalp. How was I going to cope with this exasperating boy who could absorb every scrap of my time and energy and still be out of control? Some of the residual anger and despair from yesterday hardened my feelings.

I didn't turn around when I heard the kitchen screen door

close behind me. Max sidled up to me. "How did you know? I was really quiet."

A pigeon alighted on the ridge. It was large enough to cast a distinctive shadow. I pointed at it. Max stared at it and muttered in disgust. "I wasn't scared."

"You should have been. If you fell, you could have broken your back and spent the rest of your life in a wheelchair."

He mulled this over. "Wheelchairs are fun. I wouldn't mind."

"You would if you broke your neck, lost control of your body from the neck down, had to wear diapers for the rest of your life and couldn't wheel yourself around and get up and walk away if you were bored."

He shuddered at the mention of diapers then shook his head. "That couldn't happen to me. I'm too careful."

I don't remember the rest of that day. Severe stress either imprints indelible images on my mind or fuzzes all the edges. At some point I pulled out all the files and old bank statements and tried to figure out exactly how much money I would have to generate to stay in Philadelphia without Pete. It didn't take me long to determine that I couldn't afford to stay without jobs from Pete's agency. Unlike the smaller firms in town, his agency didn't have to wait until they were reimbursed by their clients to pay their suppliers. And they paid far more. I had no other contacts for work in Philadelphia. It was too close to New York to be a big advertising town. There were three good local art schools and few jobs. The small studios and agencies hired fellow grads.

Later that week, our lawyer invited me to lunch. He was a friend of mine as well as Pete's. I assumed Pete had prodded him to call me. I told him what was going on in detail.

"You're in a bad spot. Pennsylvania law says women have to go with their husband if he's transferred or *she's* legally considered the deserter and he doesn't have to support her."

"That's sick." The knot in my stomach tightened. If it were possible to get an ulcer at twenty-nine, I was becoming a good candidate.

He made a rueful face. "Yes but that's the law in this state."

"Would he have to give me enough money to support the kids?" My mind flashed to images of my little family marooned in the bleak, dead-end world of the projects down near the airport. We wouldn't survive a week. We would have to go back to the suburbs. But what could I do there to survive? Where would Max go to school?

The lawyer was looking at me with pity. "He won't have to give you a cent. If you decide to file for divorce, by Pennsylvania law, Pete will be considered the responsible person in the marriage and he could end up with all your assets *and* the kids."

I had to clear my throat before I could speak. "Why would he want the kids? He says he loves them but he doesn't do anything to convince me that he sees them as anything more than rather irritating and constantly needy appendages. He rarely bothers to spend time with them."

"Men can be surprisingly possessive about their children. Judges don't like to give men custody but in this state, you're the bad one."

"But Pete has to work. He'd need a nanny. Why would a judge give the kids to Pete and have them raised by a nanny?"

"He wouldn't need a nanny for long. He's attractive and makes good money. Women would be lined up hoping to snag him. He'd have some woman living with him before the ink on the separation agreement was dry."

"What about Max?"

"He's a charming little boy one on one: well spoken and obviously bright. If she's around him long enough to pick up on his problems, she'll think they're your fault. Women always think they can do a better job than the first wife. Pete may go through more than one wife but there will always be *some* woman ready to jump into your shoes. When we eat lunch together women gape at him. They don't even see me."

The lawyer's comment about men being possessive jarred me. He had called that one right. Pete considered everything in our house his and his alone. He even carped at me when I used the sable paintbrushes I bought in art school, even though they still had my maiden name stamped on them. It wasn't as though I maltreated the brushes. They were expensive and I couldn't afford to replace them. I washed them with more care than I did my face.

Pete preferred his children asleep or at the other end of a phone cord. He had no prior close-up experience with children and was upset by any show of emotion other than laughter. Any human frailty made him uneasy; children whose favorite mode of expression involved exuberant shrieking and yelling literally drove him out of the house. He went to great lengths to protect himself from the messy reality of an actual family. He referred to them as *your* children. If someone asked to see a picture of his kids, he flipped open his wallet and showed them a photo of an idiotic-looking monkey. He didn't seem to understand this made most people cringe. They usually laughed and that was all he noticed. He called most days and asked what the kids had done. I did my best to turn their days into compelling vignettes. He liked this. I sometimes got the feeling this was all he wanted from his children. Touchy-feely DNA wasn't included in his genes. He couldn't help it if he tensed and flinched away from their touch. He hugged them at times, often harder than they liked, referred to them as "baby flesh" and clearly considered them his possession to be hugged or not when he chose.

They loved their father even when he pushed them out of the way as though they were objects, or gritted his teeth and glared at them. They knew there was a loving and sometimes kind man lurking inside this person somewhere if only they could find the magic words to make him appear. Innately hopeful, even I wasn't immune to this hope.

Seth brought out Pete's good side better than anyone else. He had an intuitive understanding of his father. Linda and Max used Seth to sound out their father's moods. They all agreed Seth only guessed wrong once. This was one of the rare times all three children were in accord. There was a lot of dramatic eye rolling from all three when they mentioned this but none would say exactly what had happened.

Unless one of their transgressions was too egregious to ignore, I edited it out of my daily phone chronicle to Pete. I felt vaguely guilty each time I did this but instinctively protected the children.

This was my family. No one else was going to love and protect them the way I instinctively did. No other woman would feel empathy as she supported their heads over the toilet bowl when they vomited with stomach flu then make them a towel bed on the bathroom floor and stretch out next to them so they knew they weren't alone with this misery. No one else would listen to them, watch their expressions, worry when they looked depressed or had black circles under their eyes. There was no way I would abandon them.

If I had spent the past ten years building up a name for myself, figuring out who I was and gaining the confidence in my own ability to make my own way in the world rather than raising a family I would still be in New York City and probably divorced. But I wasn't. Even if I had backed into motherhood too early for the wrong reasons, I now had a family. And they needed a mother *and* a father.

We moved to Chicago but the year without Pete underfoot had been instructive. My life was easier when he was somewhere else. He was interesting, well read and full of novel ideas. I still enjoyed being with him in short spurts but he would never again be the center of my existence. I don't know if he ever realized what he had lost. Or cared, as long as I baked a lot of pies and didn't cause a fuss.

But I didn't forget. I knew there would come a time when I

could leave Pete without harming the children. I would reconsider divorce then if my life didn't get better. It didn't get better; but it was even harder to leave when it really went downhill.

Chapter 24

I stifled my grief and did what I could to make the move to Chicago fun for the children's sake. I was polite to Pete but made it clear I thought moving was not a good idea for me or for the children. I had hopes of living in the city. Two couples with husbands who worked for the agency lived on what was called the Near North Side. Both couples had school-age children, large apartments and a Lake Michigan beach a block away. I could have dealt with that. But that wasn't what Pete really wanted.

Every family had myths. These could be acknowledged or secret. Or worst case, so deeply buried they weren't even known to their owner. Pete's myths were stuck so far inside his psyche they were just this side of China. What he said was rarely what we got.

He acted as though he liked the idea of living in the city until the house in Philadelphia was sold and I was committed to moving then he pointed out how selfish living in the city would be for the children. They should be able to walk to school without escorts and play in their own backyard just as he and I had done. He couched this myth in guilt-provoking logic. He said he had always dreamed of raising his family in a friendly town with alleys behind all the houses and parades full of boy scouts and school bands. It took me a while to figure out where the alleys and parades came from but he finally mentioned they were in a book he read as a child. For some reason, he fixated on the bit about alleys and parades as though they were the magic talismans ensuring a happy childhood.

I pointed out what seemed to me an obvious fact: living in any viable Chicago suburb put his children an hour or more away from his office. It was like Levittown with train service. I tried to convince him the children needed a father as much as they did a backyard. He said he was willing to commute so that *his* children would have *all the advantages*. It was obvious this was the only plan he was going to accept. He had already staked out the suburbs along the lake north of Chicago. We ended up in Wilmette. The town met all his criteria. It even had alleys. The lots were narrow, the houses large.

After our first winter, I figured out why the houses were so large. Even the most dedicated outdoorsman balked at outdoor activity in day after day of windy, below-zero weather. Wilmette was out of our price range but we bought a broken house hopefully referred to as a fixer-upper. Money-and-time-pit would have been more accurate. It had been on the market for almost a year. It was large, had been well built by someone with taste and money and was once well-kept. Twenty years of owners who had no clue what maintenance meant had made it unappetizing to buyers but had not destroyed the integrity of the house. It didn't have a stove, a dishwasher, or refrigerator. When prospective buyers saw the scraggly, massively overgrown greenery, peeling paint and missing roof shingles the few buyers who had shown interest decided it wasn't for them.

I had the movers crate the portrait Pete had painted of Linda and Max and tucked a couple of picture hooks and a small hammer in the bag with my nightclothes and toiletries. This crated picture went in the car. Before I even made up all the beds in the new house, I picked out the perfect spot for the picture and hung it. I would have to take it down to paint the wall but I wanted it somewhere I could see it in the meantime. I felt this picture was important: if I knew why Max had his hand clamped on his mouth, I would begin to understand a vital part of him. But he wouldn't tell me.

Because the company was moving us, real movers transported our stuff instead of our usual rent-a-truck and endless boxes of books. This was the good part.

We discovered the bad part the first time someone rang the

front doorbell and all the lights in the house dimmed. We couldn't decide whether we needed to replace the roof or the wiring first. I was more afraid of fire than leaks so we put the rewiring first and hoped for a dry month.

I had heard of Midwestern friendliness but was unprepared for the pies, cakes, cookies, lists of services, doctors and dentists and warm greetings from our neighbors. A sweet-faced woman called with forms so I could register to vote and had only Republican literature. When I asked where I could get information on Democratic candidates, she stepped back and said, "You're a Democrat?" in the same horrified voice she would have used if I had just said I had Typhoid Fever and was in the contagious stage. That's when I decided I had better not talk politics with my neighbors until they declared their party choices. The Midwest is predominantly conservative. I figured I would be a closet Liberal unless someone insisted on knowing my opinion on a touchy issue.

I enrolled Linda and Max in the grade school the following Monday. Their records had been sent as soon as I knew where we were going to live. Hopefully the six weeks left in the school year would give them a chance to meet other children their ages.

The school principal met with us before the children were sent to their classrooms. He said the Superintendent of Schools had told him he would be keeping an eye on Max's progress because Max would have the highest IQ in the school. I didn't get the impression this made the principal happy.

I couldn't blame him; it didn't make *me* happy. This burden of other people's unrealistic expectations dogged Max everywhere he went. I never did understand why so many trained educators assumed an abnormally high IQ meant Max would do everything the other kids did, only better.

The fact that overly bright people were generally regarded with appreciative awe was a mistake. Having your child labeled as super intelligent was a curse unless the kid also had the savvy and charm of a gifted politician. I supposed the two were combined in some people but Max wasn't one of them. Gifted politicians were con artists with the innate ability to read people accurately. Max was the opposite. He had no grasp of what went on in other people's minds. He was so naïve he scared me.

We were fortunate. His first grade teacher was experienced and confident enough to consider Max as an individual. She understood it was an asset that Max already knew how to read. She had her aide take him to the library to choose books and had him read to the class. For once we were lucky.

Having lived in hilly areas all my life, Wilmette was a shock. It was flat, flatter and flattest. Except when there was a high wind roiling the water, Lake Michigan was like the water in a fish bowl. It was surrounded by dune-less sand with an edge like the rim of a pie pan. From the top edge of this rise, the terrain was pancake-like to the end of the ancient lake bed where there was another slight upward tilt to the flattest terrain I've ever seen. This stretched with little variation to the Gulf of Mexico. It was dull but made it easier to spot approaching funnel clouds.

There was a Memorial Day parade with Scouts of every variety, marching bands, Veterans and fire trucks. It was so Norman Rockwell-like we were speechless. Pete smiled like a choreographer pleased with the show he had orchestrated.

The parade was followed by a neighborhood picnic. One of the two street-to-street legs of the H shaped alley behind our house ran along the side of our property. Picnic tables were set up next to our yard. Every conceivable picnic food was set out. One whole table had jellied and pasta salads, another held desserts. These were mostly frosted sheet cakes and brownies.

Charcoal grills roasted fat white sausages called Bratwurst and ordinary hot dogs. These filled the air with pungent odors. The lack of a stove and oven limited my cooking to what I could produce on a hot plate, electric fry pan that often blew fuses, or what I could cook on the grill. I opted for the grill and soaked fine slivers of diagonally sliced flank steak in soy sauce, honey, grated fresh ginger root and minced garlic then skewered these accordion-style. Like most Japanese food, it was labor intensive but I figured it was a safe bet. Everyone I knew in Philadelphia loved it.

My kids wolfed it down. Everyone else looked at it as though it were cow dung. One of the teenage boys was dared to eat it. He picked up a skewer and took a tentative nibble. His friend said, "Eeeuuu," and backed away as though he expected the meat to explode.

The boy eating the meat looked surprised. "This is real good. What is it?"

"Japanese-style barbecued beef."

The boy finished the meat on the skewer, took a second one and waved it at his friend. "I hope you don't like this so there's more for me."

A few others tried the meat and it went quickly. The main comment was that it was a little odd but good. One woman even asked me for the recipe but lost interest when I told her it contained fresh garlic and ginger root I bought in a Chinese grocery store in downtown Chicago.

Max was invited to play softball with a group of boys. He shook his head and backed away. He had retreated into an anxious silence. He was seven now but I don't think he had ever played softball.

Linda was anxious about meeting new friends but she hid it well. She was savvy enough to know finding a friend in a bunch of kids who had known each other since pre-kindergarten was going to take more than the few weeks left in this school year. She would turn nine at the end of July and would be in third grade next year. By the time girls were in third grade, the pecking order was well established. The grade school was large, had three sections in each grade and had a policy of re-mixing the individual classes every year in an attempt to forestall the inevitable cliques. I hoped this would help her find friends. There were two girls her age in our block but both went to the large parochial school on the far side of the street above ours. She jumped rope with one of these girls and bickered about the correct words to a jumping chant.

Seth watched everything with a four-year-old's bemused expression. I hovered on the edge of a group of women, listened and tried to look interested although I had no idea what or whom they were discussing. Pete stood on the edge of a clump of men talking baseball and drinking beer. He looked bored. When I went in to get a sweater, I found him sleeping on the couch. I hoped no one would notice he was gone.

When the tables and barbecue grills had all been taken home and the alley was once again swept and empty, I stood in front of the front window of the strange house and mourned the good friends I had left behind. Essentially a loner, I was polite and smiled but had an innate reserve that made it hard to form close bonds. But when I did, these friends were vital to me—they reflected and accepted me with an affirmation I thrived on, they allowed me to be uniquely myself without apology. I exchanged letters with my friend Nan, who now lived in New Haven and with Mary in Concord. They were both wonderful letter writers but I wanted more.

I hated feeling so bereft; it made me too vulnerable, too dependent on Pete. He liked this, liked me best when I needed to please him and no one else. I realized he was in for a surprise as soon as I got my feet on the ground.

Chapter 25

The beach was officially open on Memorial Day but the kids still had two weeks of school. I bought beach parking passes and the first weekday that they were on vacation we trekked to the beach. There were no people in the water. Ignoring this, Max ran full-speed into the lake. The edge of the lake was shallow and without the abrupt drop-off we were used to with ocean beaches. When the temperature of the water registered, he wind-milled his arms to avoid pitching head first into the lake. Momentum carried him about twenty feet before he could stop. Stunned, he squealed in a weird, high-pitched voice. He sounded like a whoopee pillow stuck with a pin. Fortunately, he was so shocked he was virtually breathless so only people close to him could hear the sound. I told Linda to hold on to Seth's hand, ran in after him, scooped him up and ran back out. Ice water was warmer than Lake Michigan in June.

The lifeguard sauntered over. "New to the area?" It was more statement than question. He glanced at Max, who had blue lips and a stunned expression on his face. "The lake's not much good for swimming before August. And that's if July's hot. Even then it's a waste; the bacteria count shoots up as soon as the water's over seventy-two degrees so we have to close the beach." He looked around and shrugged. "It's a nice beach for digging in sand and sun bathing...otherwise..." He smiled and sauntered back to the lifeguard stand. Teenage girls' eyes followed his progress with interest.

Max couldn't stop shaking so we went home, drank cocoa made on the hot plate and had our picnic on the kitchen floor. At least it was ant-free.

In Philadelphia, shorts and tank tops were our primary summer garb. Close to the lake in Wilmette, you could go years without feeling the need for a tank top.

The Fourth of July began with neighborhood kids riding bunting decorated bikes around the block. Small flags were distributed from a box a neighbor bought from a novelty company each year. We were just a ten-minute walk north of Central Avenue in Evanston where there was a serious parade. Seth didn't like to walk so we got out his old stroller and walked. The parade had the requisite Scouts, plus clowns, fancy cars, fire engines, six marching bands and notable personages from the area waving at us from convertibles. All the women in the cars wore hats and white gloves. The waving gloves had an old Disney cartoon feel. I had to fight not to laugh.

There were fireworks in the evening. These came from the Northwestern University football stadium. Tickets to the actual Fourth of July show in the stadium were expensive. It was supposed to be spectacular and worth the cost but I never ran across anyone who actually saw it so I couldn't substantiate this. A free golf course paralleled the lake next to the drainage canal. The neighbors told me this was the traditional place to stretch out on a blanket and watch the fireworks. The neighbors warned us there would be no parking so we loaded Seth into the stroller again and walked. There was a cold wind off the lake so we wore our winter jackets and brought hats. Wilmette was not a great place for people who worried about hat-hair.

We laid out our blanket in an empty spot north of Linden Avenue. The spectacular nine-sided Baha'i Temple rose up on the far side of the canal between our spot and the lake. Encircled by overlapping spotlights, its filigreed white stone made it glow like some swami's dream. It was a bizarre sight in Wilmette.

One of the neighbors had firecrackers he set off during the afternoon. He gave Max a bundle of sparklers and two strings of small firecrackers to set off during the fireworks. These were illegal in Illinois. He warned Max to move around when he set them off so the cops wouldn't catch him. Max was smart enough to keep these hidden until we put down our blanket and stretched out. This cheered me. Any evidence of normal street smart gave me hope.

Kids were tearing around anywhere they could find an open space. There was a constant pop-pop-pop of small strings of firecrackers. And shrieks of glee. Policemen were spotted along the sides of the golf course but they ignored the firecrackers until someone set off a cherry bomb with palpable reverberations. Two cops converged on the boys Max was watching. Max was oblivious to the approaching police. With the uncanny mistiming that became his hallmark, he picked this moment to scratch a kitchen match across the seat of his pants and light one of his strings of firecrackers. I saw this happening but was too far away to stop him. The cop confiscated the intact string of firecrackers and the sparklers and obviously asked where his parents were because Max pointed at us. The officer brought Max over and asked Pete and me for ID, which neither of us had since we had walked. He gave us a lecture about following laws and controlling our children. Pete looked at him briefly then turned away and tried to ignore him. I could see his jaw flexing as he repeatedly clenched his teeth. All around us the rising and falling sound of popping firecrackers and the occasional boom of cherry bombs continued. With each resounding bang, the cop's scowl deepened and his voice rose. He couldn't seem to stop. When he railed about parents who thought laws were made for other people, I cringed and hoped Pete didn't stand up and challenge the cop. I realized the poor man was venting his under-standable frustration. Cherry bombs could blow off fingers and blind people. He wanted to nab the person who had set it off. Instead he had a small boy with a few mini firecrackers and a bunch of sparklers.

I did my best to empathize with him but I couldn't. I felt he was attacking me. It was unfair. I didn't light off a string of firecrackers in front of him. I liked firecrackers but would have had more sense. When the policeman left and was out of earshot,

I said to Max, "If you're going to do something illegal, at least have the common sense to make sure you're not in front of a cop." My anger showed.

The man sitting on the blanket next to us looked at me with a disapproving frown. Probably a lawyer.

Chapter 26

Max's second grade teacher liked him. She had a sense of humor. When the class made paper mache topographical maps, she gave Max the want ad section so he would concentrate on the project instead of reading the news. She laughed when she told me this. "I should have known better."

"Did he make a map?"

"Not until he read every want ad. I had to explain every abbreviation. Thank God I didn't give him the personal ads. Those would have been a challenge to explain without getting fired."

She said she wanted to meet with his father. She already knew he was an artist and worked in downtown Chicago and volunteered to come in early to meet with him so he wouldn't be late for work. Pete met with her, said she just asked him about his background and family but wouldn't go into detail.

"Didn't she ask about Max?"

"Not much."

"What *did* she say?" He shrugged, turned and walked away.

Max's teacher asked to meet with me a second time. She was direct and to the point. "I've met and talked with you and your husband and now I have a question. How do you explain Max?"

"I assume you've figured out we're not responsible for the high IQ."

She laughed. "Sorry. I don't mean to insult you or your husband but I guess that's about it. Do either of you have a brilliant eccentric in your family?"

"We both had lots of eccentrics but if the few antecedents I knew were brilliant they hid it well."

"No one?"

"My dad's retired now but judging from what he did for a living, I guess he was brighter than usual. Kids aren't good at evaluating their parents objectively. He worked as a research engineer in a lab with a cyclotron. He told us how it worked so my brother and I always called it an atom smasher. We thought they were ordinary. He was asked to go to Los Alamos to work on the atom bomb when the war started, although we didn't know that until years later. His boss wanted him there but he wasn't at a high enough level to take his family so he refused."

She looked down at the table as though trying to figure out how to phrase something worrisome. "I read the headmaster's note from his school in Philadelphia. It mentioned Max's inability to follow rules." She shook her head. "No. That's wrong. He described someone who didn't even know there *were* rules. I see that. If I want him to do something, I have to give him a verbal map covering every possible permutation or he goes sideways. He's very polite but doesn't interact with the other children." She looked at me kindly. "No one wants to be paired with him because they can't predict what he'll do next. When I had playground duty, I noticed he didn't play ball with the other boys. I asked his dad if he ever played ball with Max. He looked kind of surprised at the idea but didn't answer. I assumed that was a no."

I nodded.

"What *does* your husband do with the children?"

I thought for a minute. "He takes us on long drives."

"To any place special?"

"No. He just wants to see what's down the road. We go to interesting places but we rarely stop."

By late November of 1960, the lake shore was full of thick slabs of ice piled helter-skelter on the hard frozen sand. The biting wind was a constant and cooking outside on a charcoal grill had lost its charm. It was time to get a stove. The kitchen was a small room, odd in such a large house, and had a large coat closet across one end. This was a dumb use of valuable space so I removed it.

I loved demolition. Give me a large pry bar and a heavy sledgehammer and I could rip out virtually anything. By the time the wall was gone, I had discovered an absolute rule of remodeling. The space inside every other wall might be empty but the void between the plaster walls in the part slated for removal always had plumbing, wiring and/or duct work in it. All of which had to be re-routed. I bought books on construction, wiring and home repair then went to the lumber yard and hardware store and asked questions. At first the men were politely dismissive and suggested that I send my husband in. I was small, thin and looked like a dumb kid.

When I explained I was doing the work myself and persisted, the men took me seriously and were helpful.

Pete had always dreamed of having a proper workshop so he bought a large radial arm saw, a powerful drill press and mounted a vise at the end of the large work bench already in the basement. Eventually we had every hand tool imaginable. I loved it.

An odd dynamic between Pete and me became clear in the gradual remodeling of the house. He had no problem with me doing heavy work, no ingrained sense that women weren't as capable of wielding a hammer as men and we worked together well as long as he made all the decisions. This worked for a while. He did beautiful work. I had no problem being the handmaiden as long as this got some important job done.

But he traveled a lot. And inevitably I had to make decisions on my own in order to have some bit of construction or destruction done to meet the timetable of the electrician or the plumber; the only two professionals we used. Pete rarely faulted my decisions but it seemed to threaten him to see I was so comfortable taking charge.

The electrician changed our antique fuse box to a hundred-amp circuit-breaker box and ran lines to outlets all over the cellar. He was good but expensive so I bought a book on wiring and a professional fish wire that could snake into the smallest spaces and with Max's help I rewired the entire house. He was a quick study and had small, strong hands. I just had to explain once why I had to thread the wires between floor joists, not through them, and he got it.

Pete made walnut cabinets. He did a beautiful job and seemed to enjoy working with the tools in his workshop. I worked along with him, sanded and finished wood, installed hinges and knobs, pounded thousands of ring shank nails into a plywood sub floor and installed vinyl tiles.

I saw this as an obvious need. We bought a broken house so we could live in Wilmette. We obviously had to fix it so it was habitable. I saw this as a joint effort and assumed he did too until he said, "If you think I'm going to put in this much work every time we move, think again. This is the last time I'm going to build you a kitchen."

Too amazed at his weird thinking to reply, I just stared at him with my mouth open.

***

One afternoon in March, Max burst through the back door. "Mom. Mom." I ran downstairs expecting a crisis. "Will you do it?" He shoved a crumpled paper at me. It came from Boy Scout headquarters. Eight boys including Max had signed up to be cub scouts. A den would be formed if they could find a den mother.

"You want to be a cub scout?"

"Yeah. I get to wear a uniform."

It was easy to become a den mother. One phone call indicating I was willing to take on eight second-grade boys did it. There wasn't a long list of volunteers. The boys had lessons and other commitments every other day so we ended up meeting on Friday right after school. Not the best time for a meeting. After a week of sitting still the boys were ready to roll. Eight raunchy boys shoved their way into the playroom in a testosterone cloud. The four-letter words were milder but the loud, aggressive voices sounded like Friday night at a midtown bar when the surrounding offices closed and all the unfettered males descended on it.

Second-grade boys were like a parody of masculinity. I thought they were funny but tried not to laugh. They were supposed to complete specific tasks in order to get badges. They wanted the badges. They liked the way the badges looked stitched on the uniforms and made the cubs feel like generals with long, illustrious careers. But on a Friday afternoon they weren't in the right mood to sit and plod through tasks that smacked of schoolwork.

Most kids were pyromaniacs. I used this trait as an incentive to do the badge work quickly. We lived in a forest of oak trees. Our backyard was always littered with fallen branches of all sizes. Before school shootings and terrorists, every boy carried a pocket knife and knew how to use it. I showed them how to build a small fire, how to safely carve a point on the tip of a small branch, gave each boy three extra-long fireplace matches and set out a large bowl of quartered, cored apples and a bowl of sugar and cinnamon. I spelled out the rules. These were non-negotiable. If they weren't able to get their own fire started, they had to borrow fire from another boy. If they made any aggressive moves with the sharpened stick, they would be sent home without recourse. Wilmette was a town where doors were unlocked and everyone walked so I didn't have to involve their mothers. I showed them how to stab the apples so they didn't break, how long they had to hold the speared apples in the fire to bring out the juices so the sugar and cinnamon mixture stuck then hovered over them and watched every move.

Inevitably one boy lunged at another with his sharpened stick. I took it and sent him home. He whined. "I won't do it again."

I was pleasant but didn't budge. "Good. I'll see you next week." He sulked, dragged his feet and muttered about unfairness but walked home with no further protests and showed up the next week. No one tried it again.

Most of the meetings were in our basement or backyard so I could enlist Linda's help to watch Seth during the den meetings. They were good together. Sometimes I took the boys out to the forest preserve. Linda was ten and old enough to go to a neighbor girl's house the first year I was a den leader but Seth was just five and had to come with us. Max resented having him there and went out of his way to be nasty to Seth to the point where he made the other boys uncomfortable. No matter how I handled his aggressive behavior I couldn't stop it so I hired a babysitter to take care of Seth.

Max often seemed irritated when he had to share me with seven other boys but he tolerated it. He wanted to be part of this group but he couldn't control his anger at having his brother join us. Ironically, Seth fit in well with the older boys, which might have been part of the underlying problem. Seth fit in everywhere. Max never found a situation where he felt comfortable with anyone his age. He never formed an individual friendship with any of the boys in the den.

In an era when wearing what kids called "high waters" was ridiculed, the boys wore their uniforms to school on meeting days even when their legs grew and long expanses of ankle showed below their too-short trousers. The uniform was important. It identified them as members of an exclusive tribe. This seemed to be what they all wanted.

Chapter 27

I loved museums, trains and cities. Wilmette was the last stop for what was locally called the ell. I took the three children into Chicago on the Sundays when Pete had to work or was out of town. We always sat in the front of the first car so we could see the spooky abandoned tracks and stations when the elevated train went underground and turned into a subway.

Chicago had great museums. The train ride was always a success, the cafeterias at the museums rated high but deciding what to visit at which museum was a problem. Each child had a favorite exhibit in a specific museum and the two children in what they considered the wrong museum and/or the wrong section bickered non-stop no matter what I did.

I had taken a job teaching graphics at The Art Institute of Chicago. I was to work from nine to four on Mondays and Wednesdays. A smart, kind woman named Ann Duncan cleaned and took care of children for two neighbors. She was pleased to get two more days of work and was available on the days I needed her. My classes started in early September but I hired her in mid-summer theoretically to train her but quickly saw she didn't need training. What's more, she liked Max and he liked her. After a couple of weeks, I saw she didn't need me underfoot so I suggested setting up a rotation system one day a week where I took one child at a time to a museum of their choice and the other two stayed at home with Ann.

This worked. Max loved the Science and Industry Museum with lunch at the cafeteria. Linda loved the Thorne rooms at the Art Institute with lunch at Marshall Field. Seth loved the Field Museum. He was okay with the museum food but liked it better when we ate in Marshall Field's cafeteria. He loved their rice pudding. We all hated having these special days end, Max most of all. Each time my day with him wound down, I wished I could prolong the cheerful peace we enjoyed when no one else was there to disrupt it and we did exactly what he wanted. He was so rewarding one-on-one when he wasn't bored. By the time the train arrived in Wilmette, we were both edgy and anxious. I was suddenly tired knowing the rest of my day was about to go downhill no matter what I did.

Chapter 28

Yellow jackets were mean-tempered wasps at the best of times but they were at their worst in late August. They tolerated humans earlier in the summer unless the person got between them and ripe fruit. But when the days shortened noticeably they became particularly aggressive and nasty. Theoretically insects have no understanding of death. Maybe not. But these wasps with their tiny waists and yellow and black-striped abdomens knew *something* bad was about to happen and they were royally pissed-off about it.

Our yard was 200 feet long and 50 feet wide. Absolutely flat and shaded by oak trees, it was mostly grass with a lot of weeds. A constant stream of yellow jackets flew in and out of a small hole between two flagstones in the wide patio beside the alley on the far side of the house. It was clearly a large nest. Garbage pick-up was from the back alley. Even though I was more than 30 feet away from its nest, a yellow jacket zoomed after me and stung me when I took the garbage out. I warned the kids to stay away from the flagstone patio if they went out the back door.

I was hanging curtains in the dining room when I heard voices, an odd hum then a succession of abrupt noises I couldn't identify. Thup. Thup. Thup… I finally climbed off the ladder and looked out the French door.

Max was sucking up yellow jackets with an old tube-shaped tank vacuum cleaner plugged into the outside outlet. Moving rapidly, he snagged them going in and out of the nest. He seemed to understand it was important to get every yellow jacket on his first pass. No one lives in Illinois long without learning the mean disposition of these wasps. Two boys from the house across the alley looked on. Seth stood near the stairs to the back porch on the other side of the yard. He had the intently alert expression of a deer ready to bolt.

I watched Max suck up so many insects in fast succession I was surprised they hadn't filled the vacuum. Then the hum from the motor stopped abruptly. There were no more thups. Max looked surprised then frantic as furious yellow jackets streamed out of the end of the hose. All three boys shrieked and took off running. Seth shot into the kitchen and slammed the screen door behind him. I opened the French door. Max darted in. I pushed it closed. Angry yellow jackets banged against the glass. The other two boys were only halfway through their backyard when the pursuing insects attacked. Their shrieks increased.

"The motor stopped." Max's eyes were opened wide. He was visibly jolted.

"Yeah. Big surprise. What in God's name gave you the idea to vacuum up yellow jackets? I just told you to stay away from their nest this morning. Why do you go out of your way to look for trouble? Don't you realize you could go into shock if you got stung by a lot of yellow jackets?"

"I thought I could get rid of the whole nest so we could get our bikes out of the shed. How was I supposed to know the vacuum would stop working?" He sounded aggrieved. "People shouldn't put things in the trash if they still work."

"Max, you know that's backwards. It's not their responsibility to second-guess what someone walking through the alley is going to do. You're supposed to *know* things in the trash are probably broken."

"I never saw a vacuum shaped like a long tube before. I thought it would make a good rocket. It *looks* like a rocket. I couldn't pass it up."

His offhand comment that he planned to make a rocket filled me with dread. Knowing Max I had visions of projectiles with long fiery tails shooting out of the backyard and crashing into a neighboring roof.

"Didn't you wonder why it was in the trash?" My voice rose with frustration.

"No. The lady should have put a sign on it so I knew."

"Max, you have to try to figure out *why* people do things. Like stuff is *usually* in the trash because it's broken."

"Yeah but not always. How about the clock the lady put out. It worked; she just didn't like it. You said you wished you saw it before the neighbor did."

"True. But *most* of the stuff in the trash is broken."

"How about the silver knives and forks Seth found in her trash? You still have those in the drawer."

"Okay. Do you agree that something in the trash is *more* likely to be there because it's broken than because someone just doesn't like it?"

He mulled this over and shook his head. "People around here put out a lot of perfectly good stuff they decide they don't need instead of taking it to the Goodwill. That guy in the funny old blue truck with the rusty pretend wood on the sides checks out all the alleys before the sun comes up on trash days. He fills up his truck."

"Good point. But he knew *not* to take the vacuum."

"Maybe he started on the other side of town and filled up his truck before he got to our alley. Maybe he would have wanted the vacuum if he saw it."

I gave up. Doing 'what ifs' with Max was like an endless dance with a guy who stepped on your toes no matter where you put your feet. Eventually you had to say, let's sit this one out.

Chapter 29

Max started third grade still not aware there were pecking order rules in the playground. A bunch of aggressive sixth-grade boys had been making a polio-crippled boy's life miserable during recess by daring each other to knock his crutches out from under him. They were careful to do this only when the teacher on playground duty had her back turned. No one helped the boy stand up. No one told the teacher. Anyone with sense didn't want sixth-grade bullies mad at them.

Unaware there would be consequences, the first time Max saw the nasty boys attacking the crippled boy he picked up the boy's crutches, helped him to his feet then stood next to him until the bell rang.

That day, he came home with torn pants and bloody, mud-covered knees and elbows. He mumbled that he tripped and fell then darted up to his room.

After school the following day he ran home from the wrong direction. He was out of breath and hid in his room. Linda told me what had happened. "Three sixth-grade boys followed him home yesterday and kept shoving him and tripping him. He's so dumb he helped the crippled kid again today. They were waiting for him down on Linden but he ran home another way. They'll get him tomorrow."

"Why didn't the teachers stop them?"

"Sixth-graders are too smart to get caught."

"I don't imagine it would do any good if I spoke to the teacher."

Linda just rolled her eyes, heaved a deep sigh and walked away shaking her head. She hated being linked with Max.

I called after her. "How come you told me?"

"Because they know I'm his sister. If they can't get *him*, they might come after *me*. I wish we had an ordinary name so people didn't know I was related to Max."

"Yeah, I know what you mean." I didn't realize I was talking out loud until Linda stopped and stared at me.

It wasn't an adult reaction but I shrugged and rolled my eyes. I knew how she felt. Like me, Linda liked to fade into the woodwork until she had time to check out the interactions of a new group of people. Max made this impossible for both of us. I felt ashamed of myself for cringing when someone met me and said, "You're *Max's* mother?" The shocked voice was bad enough but what really got me was when they inadvertently stepped back as though I were radioactive.

Max's teacher called the following day and asked to meet with me during lunch. Seth was in kindergarten by then so I collected him and brought him with me. She didn't waste time with pleasantries. She said, "I'd like to have Max evaluated by the school psychiatrist. He's obviously extremely intelligent but he has a problem relating to other people. He's not good at working in a group." She squinted and tipped her head as though trying to bring me into focus. "You don't seem surprised. Do you have a problem with the idea of Max getting psychiatric help?"

"No. I just wish we had enough money to get him a tutor." I tried to keep the bitterness I felt out of my voice. "He's usually good with one adult at a time."

"Yes but the real world won't come at him one by one."

She gave me the name of the psychiatrist the school used. Max spent two hours with her. He had a great time. She said she wanted to meet with me and with Max's father before she set up a treatment schedule. Pete went without his usual protests. I was surprised but decided it was best to act as though this was nothing unusual.

She spoke to us together then said virtually the same thing that the child psychiatrists had said in Philadelphia. Max was comfortable with me and freaked out by Pete. She phrased this in shrink-talk but that was the gist of it. She said she didn't feel there was any reason to see Max or me again but set up a series of appointments with Pete. He not only went to these but he actually talked with her. He said she told him he was unconsciously doing what his own elderly, remote father had done and suggested he find some activity he could share with Max.

Absorbed in his job, he didn't have the time or energy right then. He was someplace else much of the time. He came home from a month scouting locations for commercials in Hawaii. The soles of his feet were sunburned, the rest of him was deeply tanned and he had put on a few pounds. He mumbled a few platitudes about missing us but that didn't convince anyone. Not usually gregarious, he couldn't stop talking about the stunning vistas, friendly people and wonderful fruit and seafood in Hawaii.

I was depressed enough without this blithely happy, suntanned man around. I was pretty certain I was pregnant. Seth was going to begin first grade next fall and the idea of starting all over again appalled me. I felt as though I were being sucked into a bottomless quagmire.

This was eleven years before *Roe v. Wade*. You couldn't get a baby sitter and make a quick visit to an abortion clinic without anyone being the wiser. The attitude of the era and place was different. If I had had enough money to dash over to Sweden where abortion was legal, or if I had a serious medical condition that would make a pregnancy potentially deadly, or if I was carrying a child conceived as the result of rape, I would have had the procedure. But I knew myself well enough to realize even then that I would have felt haunted by a sense of loss. Once you have borne children it's impossible to think of a conceived child without investing it with a personality.

My mother was an agnostic who had brought her children up as Roman Catholics because of family pressure. She had an odd mixture of free-thinking and superstition cobbled from traditional Catholic schools in a German-speaking section of Pittsburgh, two years in a Catholic boarding school in West Virginia and a progressive public high school back in Pittsburgh. Somewhere along the line she picked up the odd belief that sex was a sinful gamble and merited penance or the threat of punishment of some sort. This was particularly true for women who had the temerity to enjoy it. She liked sex, once confiding it was the only consistently good part of her marriage with my father. She practiced birth control but never lost the feeling she might have to pay occasionally for enjoying sex by getting pregnant.

Some vestige of her odd beliefs tinged my subconscious. The familiar "what did I do wrong to deserve this" haunted me. I knew *someone's* diaphragm had to fail to account for the three or four percent failure rate but why did it have to be mine? What could I have done that was bad enough to deserve this?

I knew I would cope and even enjoy this baby but a part of me was ticking off the number of years I would have to get through before I could do some of the things I wanted to do for myself. Seven more years had just been added to this purgatory.

I had easy pregnancies. I didn't even get morning sickness. The closest I ever came to it was six weeks of vague unease if I went too long without eating. And I only had that with Max. When this sensation began with this child I was terrified. Was I carrying another Max?

Visions of another small, vibrating creature climbing out of bed night after night and sucking all my energy plagued me. Even though I knew this pregnancy might be my last chance to sleep for years, I lay awake each seemingly endless night staring at the ceiling. I saw little of Pete; we communicated with notes and phone calls. Once again, I had no idea what I should name this child. A month or so before the baby was due I got a book of baby names from the library. Names were too subjective. I picked and rejected one after another but finally decided on a short list of boy's and girl's names. I left the list on the kitchen counter where Pete couldn't miss it and asked him to circle one for each sex. He circled Matthew and Andrea.

He no longer said much about wanting six children. He was so caught up in his own life he didn't have time for the rest of us.

I arranged to have someone cover me for the few weeks I wouldn't be able to teach. There was no such thing as maternity leave in 1963. I was informed that The Art Institute only covered substitute's salaries in the case of an accident. I told the Dean this pregnancy definitely qualified as an accident but he said the insurance agency wouldn't buy this logic.

I started worrying about a baby nurse for the two days I would be working. Ann was a capable woman who wasn't fazed by Max. But adding an infant to the mix seemed a bit too much to ask. Fortunately she was thrilled at the idea of a baby to care for. She told me little babies and senile old men were the people she liked to care for most. I found this a bit scary.

When Andrea was born, the doctor checked the waiting room and couldn't find Pete. Disconcerted, he asked me where he was.

"I imagine he's at home asleep."

"How long have you been married?" The doctor sounded affronted. He called Pete.

Pete had hung out with me as much as the hospitals allowed through the first two deliveries. Their rules were pretty barbaric. With first babies, fathers were encouraged to wait at home until the mother actually went into the delivery room. Even then, husbands sat in a waiting room and smoked with other waiting fathers. When Linda was born, Pete was a nervous wreck but kept the nurses entertained because he absent-mindedly tore off the bottom of the pack and kept lighting the filter end of his cigarettes even after they pointed this out to him.

Seth's delivery was the first one where he was actually allowed to participate. He kept me company in the labor room and was asked if he wanted to come into the delivery room. When he turned gray at the offer, it was quickly rescinded.

When I went into labor with Andrea, Pete was having a bout of rheumatoid arthritis and had difficulty walking. I gathered things were becoming stressful at work. I didn't want to add to his problems so I suggested he get some sleep. Our house was only a five-minute drive from the hospital. I decided this would be easier for both of us. Unless we were talking politics or his job, we didn't have a lot to say to each other these days.

The nurse brought in the baby girl as soon as Pete arrived. She was sleeping. I was delighted when she didn't startle awake when I dropped my spoon. Maybe she wouldn't be another Max after all.

Pete looked at her. He was clearly worried about the same thing. "She's got that milk-white skin like Max but seems a lot calmer. What are you going to name her?"

"Andrea. That's the name you circled on the list."

"What list? I never saw the name before."

I started to reiterate that it was the name he chose but stopped. Why bother. By the time he came home most nights, he was operating on auto-pilot from exhaustion or a stop at a bar. He wouldn't remember and would just get irritable. "Is it okay? Do you have another name you like better?"

He said Andrea was fine but called her Andrew.

I was relieved to find the little girl loved to be hugged and snuggled and didn't mind being confined to a crib or a playpen. She was herself, not another Max.

Max seemed fond of her. He would pick her up and let her sit on his knees if she came up to him and put up her arms. He didn't actually play with her but he bought her a teddy bear with his allowance money and often watched her with a bemused expression on his face as though trying to picture what it was like to be a baby.

Chapter 30

Pete sat at his drawing board in our bedroom drawing what looked like a small house with a tree growing through its middle. Assuming it was something to do with work, I asked what the drawing was for.

"I'm going to build a tree house for the kids. I always wanted one so I could have a secret place up above everyone else that was only mine."

"Didn't you have one?"

"No. The only big tree in our yard was Ma's apple tree. I started nailing boards on the trunk so I could climb up to the crotch but she made me pull out the nails before I got the third step in place. She said she had planted the tree for fruit, not for fool kids to fall out of and break their legs."

I felt sorry for Pete. From what little I knew about his childhood, growing up in his household hadn't been easy. "That's a shame. My brother and I built one in a really old wild cherry tree on the edge of the woods below our house. We could see our house through the leaves but if we climbed up far enough, Mom couldn't see us unless she came into the woods and looked up. I used to climb up high and pretend I was invisible."

When he was satisfied with the design, Pete marked the corners and I dug holes for cement piers and the base for the ladder. I did all the yard and garden work. I was used to digging. I enjoyed pitting myself against jobs requiring hard physical effort.

Unlike Massachusetts, this part of Illinois had few stones so it would have been easy to dig four foot holes if it weren't for the many oak roots that got thicker the deeper I went. The only tool we had to cut the hard roots was the long-handled ax we used to split logs. I managed to cut the roots without difficulty for the first one-and-a-half feet but when I took a full armed swing at the next one I uncovered, I was at such an oblique angle the heavy ax skidded along the top of the root, continued through its long arc and grazed my calf. I washed the resulting skin tear, covered it with a large Band-aid and continued digging but I realized I had better ask for Pete's help with the rest of the roots. This irritated me. I hated to admit I was too small or too weak to complete any physically demanding task I started. Born hopeful and willing to try anything, I constantly fought the nagging fear I wouldn't be able to finish a project without the aid of someone bigger or smarter.

My brother, Bob, was only 21 months older than me but he was much larger. There weren't many kids in the neighborhood so Bob and I spent a lot of time playing together. He was full of wild ideas and a lot of fun but had a strong need to assert his superiority over the little sister who took his place as the youngest child in the family. Small and scrawny for my age, I spent much of my early childhood trying to prove I could keep up with him and failing because he was so much taller and stronger.

A neighbor boy sidled up to Pete when the tree house was far enough along so it was obvious the structure was built *around* a tree but not attached to it. The boy hemmed and hawed then blurted out that it was not *really* a tree house.

Pete stepped back as though aghast at this discovery and said, "Oh, my God. It isn't?"

The boy's eyes widened in alarm at this strong reaction. He looked ready to bolt but stood his ground and tried to make amends. "But it's really nice anyway."

Pete frowned and looked worried. "You really think it's okay even though I forgot the tree part?"

The boy nodded. "Yes sir, yes sir. I think it looks just fine."

Pete gave a dramatic sigh of relief, grabbed the startled boy's hand and shook it. "Thank you. That's good of you." The boy had no idea what to say. He did his best to make his mouth turn up into what was meant to be a smile but looked as though he was trying not to vomit. We didn't see much of him after that.

It was an elegant tree house. Pete had a wonderful eye for proportion and design. It became a popular meeting place for kids all over Wilmette.

Our children enjoyed it but it was never a place to hide and dream. I'm not sure private places outside are possible in the middle of a densely settled suburb full of tall oak trees where the lowest branches are level with the second story of large houses.

Chapter 31

My sister Susie and her husband gave wonderful presents. The Christmas Max was ten and Seth was seven, they gave both boys handsome brass carbide cannons that were considered safe but made enough noise to satisfy any red-blooded boy.

Both boys were delighted. I was relieved to see there was a solid chunk of brass between the explosion and the barrel of the cannon so Max couldn't use it to fire missiles. Max seemed satisfied to use the cannon as a good source of loud noise.

Two weeks later, I was in the kitchen. A noise I couldn't identify came from the basement. It was a loud whining whir that reminded me of going to the dentist when I was a child. By the time I got the tray of muffins out of the oven and opened the cellar door, the noise had stopped. I went halfway down the stairs. Max and Seth were playing pool. The only thing I heard now was the clicking of pool balls banging together and the boys arguing. They both looked at me with blank faces when I asked them if they knew what made the whirring sound earlier.

Andrea was taking a nap so I had a respite. I sat on the cellar stairs and watched the boys. The basement was large and would have had good head room if it weren't for the fat pipes carrying hot water to the radiators. The room reminded me of the German submarine at the Science Museum. The pipes and floor were painted red, the ceiling was cream colored and the walls were a glossy institutional green.

When we bought the house, the owners asked us if we would mind keeping the pool table. We were thrilled. It was in poor shape: the leather pockets were broken and sagging, the cushions were hard, and the once bright green felt was water-stained, filthy, torn and riddled with moth holes.

The table had a Brunswick tag on the underside. Pete called the Brunswick Company to have it refurbished. He was a good pool player. He hoped to share this skill with the boys. The man from Brunswick ran his hand over the battered surface as though he were stroking a desirable lover. He offered to buy it.

I was mystified. "Why? It's in terrible shape."

"Four slate tables are rare. This was built when freight was carried in horse drawn wagons." The table was expensive to fix but Pete was adamant. It turned out to be a good investment. It got a lot of use over the years. Pete's efforts to show Max how to hold the cue and where to aim ended up with Pete irritated, Max sulking and a lot of divots in the new green felt. Max was hard to teach. He hated to acknowledge he didn't already know how to do everything. He eventually learned how to play pool quite well but he did it his way.

Times when the two boys weren't fighting were rare. Seth only played pool with Max when his friend Kevin was busy. He and Max usually ended up pummeling each other. They approached everything they did together as though they were engaged in Olympic caliber competition but without the rules that kept athletes alive.

Max bitterly resented Pete's easy affection for Seth. He couldn't attack Pete so he beat up Seth on a regular basis. Two-and-a-half years older, Max was larger than Seth, and he took advantage of this and usually ended up sitting on his brother's chest. This didn't do much to forge warm, fuzzy feelings between them. One of Seth's fiercest desires was to grow larger than Max so he could beat him senseless. I tried to break them up before the first thud but they both ended up with scars.

When I went back upstairs, I left the door to the basement open. I could hear Max and Seth talking. There was urgency in their voices but I couldn't hear what they were saying. I heard the whirring noise again, so I tip-toed over to the open door and listened.

"It's getting too hot. Lemme stick it in the water and cool it off." There were ding-ding-ing sounds then a hiss. I smelled hot metal.

I could tell from the furtive quality of their voices they were doing something they didn't want me to know about. I waited until I heard the whirring noise again then slipped down the stairs so I could see them. Their backs were turned. Max was holding something against the base of the drill press. Seth was holding a plastic glass full of water. Max raised the lever on the drill press and flipped the switch to off. He was holding his cannon.

"Hey, guys." They both jumped. Seth dropped the glass, splattering both of them with water. The glass bounced and rolled under the pool table.

Max clutched his cannon. "I was just trying to make it work."

"I can see that. Let me have it. I'll need yours too, Seth."

"Why mine? I won't drill it."

"I know. But Max will take yours and drill a shaft in that."

Seth stamped his feet up the stairs muttering. "Why can't I have my own stuff? Max takes everything. He doesn't care who it belongs to."

I sympathized with him. I had considered putting a lock box in their room so Seth could keep his treasures separate but I knew this was futile. Max would just figure out a way to pick the lock. He didn't acknowledge the idea that Seth and Linda had the right to their own possessions. This made both of them crazy. Linda screamed and ranted when he rifled through her belongings. Seth just found hiding places for his. He was creative. It wasn't unusual to find his stuff in odd places like the inside of the piano no one played anymore. But no matter where he had them hidden, Max usually found them.

Seth *did* have one advantage. He wasn't afraid of spiders. Max shuddered at anything creepy-crawly so Seth stashed some of his things in a metal pretzel tin under the spider infested back porch. This worked until the open area under the steps was snowed in.

I hid both cannons. Max worked hard to find them, going through my belongings regularly. I knew he wouldn't give up. I also knew he had no idea how my mind worked. This was one of the few times I saw this as an asset. Pete insisted I should just pitch both cannons in the trash, but I couldn't do that. They were beautifully made and they were a present from my sister and her husband. At some point both boys would treasure them.

We had a neighbor whose name was Dan. We called him the Pied Piper of Wilmette. He had a beautiful wife with a dry sense of humor and a charming little boy but he hated what he did for a living. Unfortunately, he was exceptionally good at it and made a lot of money. He dreamed of being a cowboy but ended up as the best house painter in Wilmette so he entertained himself by describing his wild youth to adoring boys. Every boy within walking distance wanted to hang out with him.

He made stealing dynamite from work sites and blowing it up down at the beach in the off season sound like the ultimate adventure, something every red-blooded boy should be doing in his spare time. He told the boys harrowing stories about *almost* getting caught by the police. In his world no one ever blew off parts of his fingers, lost an eye or got more than a stern lecture from a stodgy father if someone turned him in and the police came calling. He didn't seem to be aware that stealing dynamite was now a Federal offense. A felony; not a boyish prank. He and Max talked guns and explosives for hours.

I have often wondered if our life would have been easier if Dan had been interested in playing a musical instrument or collecting stamps. Probably not. Some behavior is clearly inbred. Max seemed programmed to love anything with the potential to explode or shoot projectiles.

Chapter 32

Our good friends Wing and Pearl had moved to Chicago around the time Andrea was born. They were part of the California contingent working for the agency in Philadelphia and had been our friends and neighbors in Levittown. Wing had frequently stayed at our house in downtown Philadelphia when he and Pete worked late.

Wing's and Pearl's parents and siblings lived in California; mine were spread all over the country. Our four children and their three children had a natural affinity for each other. We formed a chosen extended family and celebrated all holidays and birthdays with them. Dedicated to good food, we had cook-outs, explored exotic recipes and went on picnics. Max felt at home with them and they were so familiar with him, they were never surprised by his unique point of view or his outlandish behavior.

One of our joint activities in warmer months was fossil hunting. The remains of numerous coal mining operations formed distinctive hills on the flat prairies south of Chicago. These weren't hard to find if you knew where to look. Years of rain had washed dirt off the heaped mine tailings, exposing smooth oval stones. When they were split open the stones revealed fossil impressions of ferns and leaves that looked like stippled pen and ink drawings. Most of the fossils we found were just fragments suggesting the original form but a rare few revealed a complete image. These were treasured and kept us fossil hunting.

Because the soil had been dug from far below the surface, it had virtually no nutrients in it. Grasses and other prairie plants grew only in small fissures where bits of vegetation had lodged and rotted. With virtually no ground cover to hold the soil in place and soak up moisture, even the smallest amount of rain turned the mine tailings into thick muck that made scaling the hills difficult and digging impossible.

Fossil hunting was a project for clear July and August days. Hot ones. Wing and Pearl always brought a cold watermelon in a large cooler. Born and raised in California, they both knew how to pick out perfect melons. We loved eating the sweet, icy fruit and spitting seeds at each other. There's something about having permission to spit watermelon seeds at anyone within range that wipes out normal boundaries.

Linda and Seth tried to find good fossils but Max was only minimally interested. Andrea was carried around until she was old enough to stop eating stones. One day, after the picnic part of the outing, Max gave a whoop of delight and started picking up what we assumed were stones and stuffing them into his backpack. He walked back and forth with his eyes on the ground with an occasional abrupt stop to swoop and grab. I was pleased to see him so involved in what the rest of us were doing. I kept an eye on him. The terrain was open so I could see him clearly. He was only looking at the ground immediately in front of his gaze. There was a possibility he would blindly stumble on the remains of a mine opening or a sink hole.

I yelled at him to stay on the path but he was too engrossed in finding stones to pay attention to what I said. I was watching him and mentally marking his position, afraid a sink-hole would suddenly suck him into the ground and rescue time would be crucial.

Pete and Wing were cracking open stones. They had an unusually large stone propped against a heavy mica-studded boulder and were trying to decide where Pete should place the pointed edge of the cold chisel so Wing could tap it with the hammer. You only got one chance. With stones like the one the two men were studying, tapping the right white line on the end might reveal a perfect Gingko or fern leaf. Tapping the equally attractive line a fraction of an inch away might reveal a portion of a non-descript piece of bark. They finally decided to go with the larger white line.

I was momentarily distracted. When I glanced back at Max, he was in the process of latching his backpack closed so he didn't lose his stones. He turned, ran across to the hill we were on and grabbed the edge of Wing's shorts a second after Wing tapped the cold chisel revealing a clump of bark pieces. Wing shrugged and looked at Max.

Max was so excited, it took a second to figure out what he was saying. "Wing! Wing! Look what I found." Face flushed, he dumped out the contents of his backpack: empty shotgun shells.

Wing stifled his shock and said, "Amazing, Max! Where did you find so many?" Then he bent down, picked up a few shells and looked at them closely. "These are different sizes. Do you think they came from different shotguns?"

Thrilled with Wing's interest, Max rattled off a scary stream of facts about shotguns. He sounded as though he were quoting from a fire arms manual.

Chapter 33

Max was in fifth grade when Cub Scouts ended and he decided he wanted to be a Boy Scout. There was an active troop in Wilmette but the current scout master was about to retire and move to Arizona. Notices had been sent to all scout parents asking for a volunteer.

Pete had left the Philadelphia-based agency six months earlier. Two years after we joined him in the midwest, he was bored with the account that had triggered his imperative need to move to the Chicago office. He tried working as an account executive for the agency on a different account but that turned into a disaster so he quit and freelanced for six months. He had started talking about California. I was expecting him to announce another move but he was offered a job with a large Chicago agency and had the sense to take it.

The new agency encouraged civic spirit and made a point of sending artists and copy writers home at a decent hour. The agency's founder was a big supporter of the Boy Scouts. So Pete volunteered to be the new scout master. He said this would be a good way to do something meaningful with Max. Pete had only vague ideas about scouting. He had never been a boy scout himself but he had always liked camping. Max was thrilled.

Being a scout master took a lot of commitment and an enormous amount of time. There was management training, an introduction to scouting traditions, camping skills to learn so they could be taught, monthly camp-outs, a once-weekly meeting at a local church and accompanying the troop during the two weeks when the bulk of the troop went to camp in Wisconsin.

Pete took the job seriously and became an expert at scouting and camping. Our vacations for the next few years were one week at what was called family camp where I had the use of a comfortable cabin on the family side of a Wisconsin lake. Pete and Max were with the troop at the large scout section on the other side of the lake. Family camp included two excellent meals cooked by someone else, a beach for swimming and a chance to do a lot of reading while the younger children played under supervision. I enjoyed these weeks and missed them when the children's activities became so varied we couldn't go anywhere in a clump.

Pete continued to spend virtually every weekend and all his vacations at scout functions. Max and later Seth went on all the camp-outs and had calamity stories that could have given a stand-up comedian an evening's worth of great material. On average there were 60 boys in the troop and most went along on every camp-out, whether they were sick or well.

The initial idea that Pete and Max would bond through scouting was lost early on. Max was proud his father was the scout master but he said there was a downside. In the midst of every calamity the only name Pete could always remember with enough certainty to shout was MAX! Their relationship was as far from one on one as possible. Now Max had to share his father with 60 other boys.

Wilmette was a classic high-end suburb. A large percentage of fathers worked long hours and traveled. Pete became the father figure for quite a few of the boys in the troop. We always had scouts underfoot. They showed up as soon as school let out and always seemed surprised and a bit put out to discover Pete was still at work or out of town. This became a family joke. But Max wasn't amused.

The psychiatrist's belief that Max and Pete would bond if they did something meaningful together influenced them both. Max went on every camping trip full of hope that *this time* things would be different: his father would show him some sign of affection or notice and applaud something he had done well. Pete felt guilty because he could be patient with other boys but not with Max. They both came home from camping trips exhausted, moody and barely speaking.

Chapter 34

The summer Max was eleven and Linda was thirteen, Pete came home with two excellent books: *What Every Boy Should Know About Sex* and its companion book, *What Every Girl Should Know About Sex*. Seth was nine that summer and Andrea was two.

Linda read her book and agreed it was interesting. Max read his and Linda's books. With the information gleaned from the two books, he wanted to check out the specifics of female anatomy. He had been bathed with Linda when they were babies and they had each made cursory checks of their physical differences then. He had seen me change Andrea's diapers recently and often saw her running around the house unabashedly stark naked but he hadn't really paid much attention to the close-up geography of female genitals.

When he asked Andrea if he could look at her bottom, she was happy to strip naked. Linda and Seth watched the viewing. Neither thought it unusual. Nor would I have if I had seen them. But Max was on the edge of puberty and felt sexual stirrings. He didn't realize then that this reaction didn't mean he was a sexual deviant and had the hots for his baby sister: unexpected erections were going to be a constant all through puberty and could be triggered by anything and everything.

Andrea liked the attention. She thought it was a new game, sort of like playing doctor with the big kids. When she asked Max if they could play the naked game again, he panicked, yelled at her and threatened bodily harm if she ever mentioned it again. He was certain he would be in trouble if Pete or I knew about it. I don't know why. Pete had just gone to the trouble of buying him a user-friendly, explicit book about sex and I had been telling him since he was very small that his penis belonged to him and he could do whatever he wanted with it as long as he wasn't embarrassing someone else or infringing on their rights.

But sex is complex and I had no control over what other people told him. He was suddenly afraid of Andrea, blamed her for his hormonally triggered reaction, decided he hated her and wanted her out of his life.

I saw the change in his attitude toward her but had no clue at the time what had triggered his hostility. I've often wished Max had told me what had happened then instead of when he was 30. I could have reassured him his curiosity about gender specifics was normal. The incident had been so unimportant in Andrea's mind that she quickly forgot about it and had no clue why Max was suddenly so nasty to her. His viciousness was mostly verbal threats to hurt her in terrifying ways and an occasional arm twist, never when Pete or I were around.

Andrea ended up afraid of him. I think we all were. He had always been nasty and imperious with Seth. I assumed this was an unusually strong case of sibling rivalry. But it was particularly unsettling to watch him turn on the only sibling he had seemed to like. What could a baby have done to rouse such hatred?

I was doing a lot of freelance artwork at the time. This was difficult during the summer when Max wasn't in school. I tried to pick up and deliver work on the days Ann was there but it didn't always work out that way. Ann worked Mondays and Wednesdays all year round. I knew Andrea was safe with her. One of my clients decided he wanted a piece of finished art on Tuesday instead of Wednesday. I couldn't tell a client I wouldn't be able to deliver artwork because I was having problems with child care. The only baby sitter available on Tuesday was an older woman who coped well with everyone but Max so I took him with me.

I decided he would be able to keep out of trouble if he brought a book and I gave him exact parameters. He was pleased to be alone with me. I counted on this as an incentive for him to behave. The client was anal but we had gone over the art in such minute detail during the last two visits, I assumed I could drop off the work quickly. This hope vanished before I even got in to see him. He kept me waiting for the better part of an hour, enough time for Max to discover he didn't like the book he had brought. He would read it since he always finished any book he started, but it wasn't going to keep him from exploring.

We were about 18 miles north-west of Wilmette in a low building set in the middle of fields of soybeans. In the distance a line of trees snaked across the horizon. This was usually an indication there was a creek meandering through a dip in the landscape. There was a slight roll to the ground, not something I would have noticed if I were in Pennsylvania or Massachusetts but after five years in Illinois I saw even the most subtle rise in the terrain. Hopefully it would seem so dull to Max, even a disappointing book would keep his attention.

When I finally got into the client's office, he insisted we go over the artwork again in minute detail. This was nothing more than his need for absolute control. He needed the art a day early because the printer insisted this was the only way he could print and ship it in time to distribute the information at a convention in Salt Lake City. I knew there was no question of a redo. He stayed seated. I had to stand and hang over his oversized desk to see what he was talking about.

A sudden movement outside the large window behind him startled me. A head popped into view and disappeared so quickly I wondered if I had really seen it. It popped up a second time, this time far enough so I could see Max's grin. Then again. This time, he was holding something in his hand. He was trying to show me what it was. I frowned at him and shook my head. The client looked up before I could shift my eyes back to the drawings. He swiveled around, looked out the window then turned back to me a fraction of a second before Max's head re-appeared.

I could feel sweat prickling my back.

"Is there something outside?"

"Just a bird with red on its wings. We don't see those in Wilmette."

He shrugged. "Red-winged blackbirds. They're everywhere here."

Thank God I didn't describe some exotic bird he'd want to see for himself. I forced myself to keep my eyes on the paper. It wasn't easy. I had good peripheral vision. I flinched when Max tried to bang the window with whatever he was holding. This time the client frowned and started to turn around. Frantic to keep him focussed on the art, I pointed to a picture I had enlarged. "This was the size you wanted. You were right. It does look better."

By the time he accepted the work and gave me an invoice to submit, I was shaking.

"Are you cold?"

I couldn't say yes. Sweat was dripping into my eyes. I said the first thing that came into my mind. "Yes but a few seconds ago, I was burning up. Is there some kind of virus going around your office? I felt fine until about fifteen minutes after I sat in your reception room."

Fortunately he didn't know much about viral incubation times. He scooted his chair back as far away from me as he could and tried to talk without inhaling. "We do have three people out sick. I hope you're going to be all right."

"Thanks. Me too." I managed a brave smile and bounded out as quickly as I could without breaking into a run. I figured he wasn't going to offer to walk me out. He was probably in the men's room scrubbing his hands raw before I got to the front door.

Max ran around the corner of the building. He was clutching a bulging paper bag. "The lady said I could have as many as I could pick. She said they're apricots."

"Great. Let's get out of here. I'll tell you why as soon as we're out of sight." I started up so fast I spun gravel. Not easy with a

VW bus with a 35 horse-power engine.

As soon as the plant disappeared in the rear-view window, I told Max why it was hard on me when I took him someplace where it was important for him to behave and he didn't do that. I could hear my voice shifting from reasonable to strident. I forced myself to stop railing at him. I had to constantly remind myself he could be hurt by my criticism even though it never changed what he did. I was stupid to bring him with me. Expecting him to stay put and wait patiently was as reasonable as staking out a terrier and assuming it wouldn't bark. It didn't do any good and it just left us both feeling frustrated and wronged. I took a deep breath. "How did you know which room I was in?"

"I just started at one end of the building and checked each window. Why do people with big windows always sit facing the door?"

"Do they all do that?" I was hopeful. Maybe no one saw him.

"All but the lady who told me about the apricots. She had her window open and came over and talked to me. She asked what I was doing. When I said I was trying to find you, she told me where she thought you would be then asked if you make jam. She's nice. She asked me to pick all the apricots I could reach so they didn't go to waste. She said she was glad someone still made jam. She gave me the bag."

He turned to me. "How come you kept frowning at me when I was trying to get your attention while you were talking to that man?"

"I was trying to signal you to stop jumping up at the window."

"Why? I wasn't hurting anything."

"No. You weren't. It's because the guy I did the work for would be freaked if he saw you."

"That's dumb. What difference would it make?"

I sighed. My impassioned explanation of exactly what he did

wrong and why had slid right by him. I sometimes wished I could look inside his head and figure out how he processed what I said. "It's called being unprofessional. If I have the temerity to have kids and work, I'm supposed to keep them invisible." I had to explain what temerity meant.

He mulled this over for a few seconds then said, "That's dumb. Ladies are supposed to have kids."

"Not if they want to work in my business."

When I pitted the apricots I discovered some of them had small apricot-colored worms in them. Max offered to help pit the fruit. I showed him the worms. "Watch for these and pick them off." His face twisted with revulsion. He hated bugs. Seth was sitting next to him and noted the reaction. He pitted an apricot, took out the worm, held it up so he had Max's full attention then very deliberately put it into his mouth, swallowed it and stared at Max with his eyebrows raised in an unspoken challenge.

Max gulped, shuddered, pitted the small fruit until he found a worm, put it into his mouth and swallowed it. His face went pale. Involuntary tears filled his eyes. He gagged but kept himself from vomiting with sheer power of will.

Seth looked surprised. He pitted apricots until he found another worm and swallowed it. Max looked sick. He was sitting on a stool with no back. I hoped he didn't faint and crack his head on the radiator behind him. His hands were shaking. He found a worm and swallowed it.

Seth knew he had an advantage. Eating worms wasn't his idea of fun but he had a strong stomach. Fascinated, I watched the merciless duel. How would it end? There were a lot of apricots. They finally quit.

Seth gracefully allowed Max the last worm then said, "This is boring. I'm going over to Kevin's house."

Neither boy ate the apricot jam I made.

Chapter 35

Later that summer, Pete came home with three bags of candy and a bag of licorice sticks. He got three large bowls out of the cupboard, filled one with jelly beans, one with cellophane-wrapped sour balls and one with wrapped peppermint kisses. He picked through the glasses until he found a heavy one and stood the licorice sticks in it.

Bemused, I said, "Are we having company?"

"Nope. I like having candy around the house. I just decided the kids are old enough to leave it alone."

"What made you think that?"

"When I was their age we had candy out in bowls."

"There is no *their age*. Linda is fourteen, Max twelve, Seth ten and Andrea is three. You can't keep candy out and expect all of them to leave it alone."

"Why are you always so damn negative? If I tell them to leave the candy alone, they will. Normal families keep candy out."

"Their dentist is going to love you."

Pete put the candy in the living room and family room then helped himself to a handful of jelly beans and went in search of the children so he could explain the candy rules. One by one the kids appeared in the kitchen and asked me why their father suddenly decided to leave candy out on the tables.

"He likes having candy around."

A few minutes later Linda came into the kitchen with something large in her mouth. When she talked around it I realized she was sucking on a red sour ball. "How come Dad bought spice jelly beans? Fruit ones are better." The pockets of her shorts bulged.

Andrea brought me a peppermint kiss and asked me to unwrap it for her. I took it away from her. "You can't have these or the sour balls Andrea. You might choke on them." I took a small box of raisins out of the cupboard over the refrigerator and gave that to her.

She thanked me but looked disgusted. "Which of the candies *can* I eat?"

"What did your dad say?"

"He said just have a little bit of candy after we eat our dinner. I ate everything on my plate. Why can't I have candy instead of raisins?"

"Because raisins are good for you. Candy isn't."

"If it's not good for us, why did Dad buy it then?"

"He wants us to be normal."

"What's that?"

"The best of all possible worlds."

She rolled her eyes.

I put the bowls of sour balls and peppermint kisses up too high for Andrea to reach.

When Pete got home from work the following day, except for a few purple jelly beans, the candy bowls were empty. He stacked the bowls and brought them into the kitchen. "Why didn't you refill the bowls? The only way we're going to teach the kids to eat reasonable amounts of candy is to have it available all the time so they don't think it's something special."

"I didn't refill them because I still don't think it's a good idea to keep candy around all the time."

"Just because you grew up in a weird house where no one ate candy doesn't mean your kids shouldn't eat it."

"What makes you think we didn't eat candy? Dad loved it. He used to make fudge when he was in the mood and he always kept bags of peanut butter kisses and jelly beans around. When I was in high school he started buying M&Ms."

"You don't like M&Ms."

"I liked the chocolate part. I just didn't like the covering. And it was too much trouble to soak the covering off and dry them. It was easier to walk down to the corner and buy a Hershey almond bar when I wanted chocolate candy."

Pete frowned at me. I think he was trying to decide if I were joking or not but decided he didn't want to know. I wasn't but I only tried it once and found the funky taste of the coating stuck to the little chocolate insides.

Pete brought home bags of candy for the next few weeks. By then the house was infested with tiny sugar ants. Not trusting the sudden surfeit of free candy, Max and Seth had been stashing candy in their rooms. The wrapped candy didn't attract ants but Pete kept buying the spice jelly beans. The kids didn't like them but they kept putting them in their mouths just long enough to be certain they *really* didn't like them then taking them out of their mouths and putting them into their pockets, onto the closest piece of furniture, or into the nearest wastebasket. The candy company should have sold their flavorings to the outfits that made ant traps. They would have had a winner. I think we were attracting ants from every suburb on the north shore of Chicago.

Without comment, Pete stopped buying candy. I felt sorry for him. He had all these mental images of what normal families did but he couldn't seem to grasp that this mythical perfect family existed only in his dreams. His ideas of what made a happy household were irritating but so lame they were oddly touching.

He didn't grow up with a good teacher. Pete's father was a remote man, the age of most children's grandparents when Pete was born. I only met him once before he died. Hospitalized, he had suffered a series of mini-strokes so his mental capacity was altered but he appeared to be fully cognizant when I met him. Old and frail, he was still a handsome man with a shock of thick white hair, a sharp nose and still vividly blue, assessing eyes. Pete's eyes.

The youngest of nine children, Pete's dad barely knew his own father. A sea captain/ cargo ship owner on the China to Provincetown run, the man was never home for more than six months at a time. Much of that time was spent in Boston offloading the China goods and getting cargo for the next trip. I gather he brought his children hard candies from Boston. So Pete's father did the same thing with his children. This was Pete's happiest memory of his father and he wanted to pass on the pleasure he had enjoyed.

Chapter 36

I heard the front door close. Then footsteps on the stairs. It was dark. The clock next to the bed said 1:12. I pulled on a robe and opened my bedroom door. Max and Seth were creeping up the stairs jostling each other, breathing hard and trying not to laugh. There was just enough ambient light to see they were naked except for their white underwear and sneakers. My bedroom was on a separate hall. I closed the door behind me then waited for them. They were so absorbed in whatever they had done they didn't notice me in the dark hall. I followed them into their room and flicked on their bedroom light. Seth gave a startled squeak when he saw me. Max jumped at the sudden light but looked pleased. Seth looked embarrassed.

"So, where have you been in your skivvies?"

They looked at each other, their faces equally guilty then Max straightened and assumed the challenging bravado stare I was seeing more and more. "Out."

I knew I had to be careful here. "Did anyone see you?"

"No. We were quiet."

Seth didn't contradict Max but was clearly worried.

I looked at him. "Did any lights come on? Or dogs bark?"

Seth flicked a nervous glance at Max then said, "Yeah. The lady on Eighth Street turned on her bedroom light and looked out when her dog started barking. I think she called the cops. A patrol car drove down the street a couple minutes later. We heard it coming so we hid in a basement stairwell in the house near the other end of the alley. After the cop went back to the lady's house I wanted to go home but the bet was…"

"This was a bet?"

Max did his macho look again. "We each bet our allowances. I said we could walk around the whole block in our underwear without getting caught. Seth bet his allowance we couldn't. I won."

"How about the lady calling the cop? Wasn't that sort of getting caught?"

Max looked indignant. "No way. The cop never saw us."

"But the lady's dog heard you and she looked out. Are you sure *she* didn't see you? She wouldn't bother to call the cops just because the dog barked. That dog barks if a squirrel walks by."

Seth was looking hopeful. Max was uneasy but defiant. "Even if the cop saw us, it was no big deal. We weren't doing anything wrong. People wear bathing suits out in public that cover them a lot less than underwear. "

"True but they wear bathing suits at the beach. People expect to see them there. They don't expect to see boys wearing underwear in their backyard. Then it might feel scary. And you might have been trespassing on a lot of people's property. You were definitely disturbing the peace if the lady was upset enough to call the police. That's three things. How did you get out without me hearing you?"

"Out the window. We climbed on that little roof over the front door then held on to the roof braces." Max looked proud. "I do it all the time."

I decided not to acknowledge this comment. "The bet was all the way around the block? Right?" Both boys nodded. "So you made it halfway without being caught?" Max was looking angry. Seth was looking hopeful. "Okay. So you each half-won. What was the penalty if you didn't make it all the way?"

Max glared. "I give him my allowance."

"So you both won and both lost. How about we call it a draw? Seth gives you half of his allowance and you give him half of yours."

"That's not fair. Then he'll end up with some of my money. My allowance is more than his." He was flapping his arms with frustration as though he wanted to hit someone but couldn't decide whom to hit first.

I frowned. "Yes. That's true."

Seth looked at me. He knew I had just dumped the issue in his court. He was smart. He had to share a room with Max. He shrugged. "That's okay, Max. You can keep all your allowance. I had fun."

I knew I had to separate the boys. Max had a need to control Seth. Max did what he wanted to do without any indication that he had any understanding of the possible consequences of his actions. Seth did know the consequences, yet he not only followed Max's lead and ended up involved in things that he knew were self-destructive, he sometimes taunted Max, knowing his brother would do anything to prove he was superior.

I had an older brother who did his best to control me but by the time I started grade school, I had figured out I would never be able to fly and stopped leaping out of trees and jumping off porch roofs no matter what my brother said.

Max was in eighth grade. Seth was in fifth. They were in different schools. If it weren't for their competitive love/hate relationship, they would have had little to do with each other. Pete was as confused by their relationship as I was. He and his brother had the same age difference between them as our two boys did, had nothing in common and avoided each other, although the avoidance might have been mostly on Pete's part.

A friend of his told me the older Max made a point of intruding when a bunch of Pete's friends were just hanging out laughing and trading jokes. The older Max had the ability to chill any cheerful gathering and made Pete and all of his friends feel stupid and gauche.

I decided moving Max to his own room might help. The house in Wilmette had a full attic with a narrow stairway in the hall closet. It took me the better part of a year but I built two rooms in the attic with a knee wall and storage on both sides. The house was a classic Dutch colonial with a large wing on the back. I made full use of Pete's tools and added a few of my own. I had to hire a plumber to put in radiators, a sheet rocker to hang the drywall and a man to put down carpeting, but I was able to do the rest of the work by myself. I ended up with a few more books on construction and knew all the men in the hardware store and lumber yard by name.

Buying the steel circular stairway was entertaining. I had gotten specification sheets for pre-made circular stairs at the lumber yard and drawn up exact plans. The stairs were manufactured at a company located in an industrial section of South Chicago. I dressed the way I usually would to go into town, in a good suit, stockings, heels, perfume, the whole lady-going-to-town rig. I should have shown up in overalls, work boots and poured sawdust over my head. A little BO might have helped.

They made me sign an agreement saying I would accept the stairs without argument and I had to pay the full amount before they started making them. When I drove back down to pick up the stairs, I wore jeans and work boots but it didn't help. There was a lot of head shaking. Everyone in the company, even the gray haired bookkeeper came out to the loading dock to watch the men fitting the pie-shaped pieces into my VW bus.

Pete, Max and Seth helped me set up the stairs. It was like playing with a very heavy construction kit. The sections fit together perfectly. I was the only one not surprised.

Between his job and the Boy Scouts, Pete was busy. On the rare evenings he was free, fortified by a few drinks, he would go up to the third floor and check out the progress. He never said much, yet he managed to make me feel like a not too bright kid. I imagine some of my reaction came from left-over feelings from my critical father who was good on disapproval and totally lacking in praise, but it wasn't all my imagination.

Pete sometimes repeated his weird saying about me squirting out around the edges each time he thought he had me under control. I found this creepy; it made me feel like a bug with a big thumb holding me down. If I asked him why he said it, he would

162

look at me with a blank expression. I wasn't sure if he realized what had just come out of his mouth.

***

Max moved into the third-floor room. It didn't occur to me to ask Seth if he wanted to move into the third floor bedroom or stay in the old one. To me, the large, well lit second floor room was clearly the better choice but Seth took it as another indication Max was the more loved child because he got the new room. The odd dynamics between the two brothers still popped up but less so. Seth had been in a lifelong war with Max to establish his own turf. His life was a little better but he still had to go to Kevin's house if he wanted to play games or even just talk about subjects that interested him without Max interrupting him and telling him he was stupid.

Max wasn't able to acknowledge anyone else's right to have a conversation he didn't dominate. With Max you listened to what he wanted to say or you left the room. I sometimes hung out in my bathroom if I wanted to read.

Chapter 37

One day I heard a motor-bike stop in our alley. I could see feet through the cellar window. One pair belonged to Max but I didn't recognize the other ones. I was in the kitchen staring into the refrigerator, hoping an idea for supper would leap out, when the front door knocker clacked. A police car was idling in the alley, a uniformed officer at the door. A red motor-bike was parked in front of the squad car.

The officer handed me a paper detailing ownership of a motor-bike. "He's underage, ma'am. He can own a motor-bike but he can't take it off your property. It's a shame you don't live out in the country. Lots of kids there drive around on trails they make."

I wondered if I looked as dumbfounded as I felt. "He owns a motor-bike? Since when?"

The back door slammed. Max bounded into the living room. He answered me. "I bought it from a kid at school."

The officer tried to look stern but it was a losing battle. He was young and he clearly empathized with Max. "Just keep it in your own yard, Max. If you have any friends with a farm, maybe your mom would haul the bike in your van. It'll fit."

The officer touched his hat in a salute. He left me with the feeling I was inadequate because I didn't own a farm so my 14-year-old son could ride his motor-bike around. I didn't even know anyone who owned a farm.

I remembered that summer as the motor-bike summer. Max had been saving all the money he earned for months. I never learned why the boy sold the bike. Max had all the proper papers, duly signed over to him. I felt pathetically grateful for this brief indication that Max was trying to follow the rules.

We had a long backyard with a cement walkway that split at the garage. One strip went behind the three-car garage; the other went to the large cement area in front of the three doors. Max drove the bike back and forth. I stood at the back door watching. Each time he got to the place where the walk divided, he checked to see if I was watching. It was like the marble steps on Pine Street in Philadelphia all over again.

I knew I was in trouble.

Friends told me I should insist Max sell the bike. I know that made more sense for me. But I tried to consider it from Max's point of view. He hadn't had many successes. Owning a motorbike was a tangible one. His father agreed. He saw wanting wheels as a boy thing. He said it was hard on kids to have to live by rules that didn't exist when he was Max's age.

The police officer had told Max the parameters. I had to help him stay within them. But I knew Max would test and retest the limits. I had to figure out a way to look out the back door hour after hour without going crazy from boredom. I got out a braided rug I had begun three years ago. It was about three feet by four feet. I worked on it in front of the French doors looking out at the backyard. I kept the overhead light on so I was instantly visible from anywhere in the yard.

A woman whose garage opened into the alley was afraid she would inadvertently back into Max as he buzzed past her driveway. Or that was what she said. Other than during the long motorbike summer I never saw her. She was always polite but may have hated kids. If I left the dining room window, even for a few minutes, Max roared down the alley, wheeled around in the middle of Eighth Street and went back to the apron in front of our garage. When the woman saw him do this, she called the police.

I suspected most of the officers empathized with Max. He was never cited, even though they were called a couple times a week. Max said a lot of them had Harleys and they talked about motorcycles. One of them had an Indian. Max was delighted when *he* showed up.

The other kids bitterly resented the time I had to devote to Max in my effort to keep him out of the alley.

One day Linda said, "Why's Max the only one you care about? Why aren't the rest of us important?"

Each time I heard this, I felt the same frustration. What more could I do to let them know they were not only loved but appreciated for being themselves? Their feelings were certainly justified. I asked Seth if he felt the same way. He just looked at me as though I were a bit dim. "Of course. When he's around, we might as well not be alive."

I decided to send Max to Boy Scout camp for an extra two weeks. The relief in the house for the month he was gone was wonderful but this brief taste of normalcy made it even harder to cope with him when he came home. He was like a dog that barked all the time. It took a while before I could get used to him being around and selectively tune him out.

We joined a hunting and fishing club and hauled the bike up to it whenever possible. It wasn't our property but it was private land so we got permission for Max to ride back and forth. Each time we went there, I hoped he would ride the bike inside the yard for a while but it didn't work that way. If anything, the freedom to ride all over the fishing club whetted his appetite for the open road.

By the end of September, the braided rug had grown to room size. I was running out of wool strips and I was afraid my hands would end up permanently curled into claws from bending the wool into neat braids.

Then one day the motor-bike was gone. Max said he had sold it to a guy at school and made a profit. I complimented him on his savvy business sense and breathed a sigh of relief. I should have held my breath.

Chapter 38

One afternoon, not long after Max turned 15, I heard an unmistakable sound coming from his room. I grew up around guns. I knew exactly what a 22-caliber sounded like when a shell was ejected. I tore up the stairs and into his bedroom so fast that Max didn't have time to hide. He was crouched, aiming out the window at something across the alley.

"WHAT IN GOD'S NAME ARE YOU DOING WITH A GUN?" I shrieked with a combination of panic and frustration.

He clutched the gun as though he held a priceless treasure and I was a marauding Mongol. "I thought you went to the grocery store."

"I DIDN'T ASK YOU WHERE YOU THOUGHT I WENT. I WANT TO KNOW WHERE YOU GOT THE GUN."

"I bought them from a guy at school. I used my motor-bike money for them. I don't have bullets..."

"WHAT DO YOU MEAN YOU DON'T HAVE BULLETS? I HEARD THE SHELL EJECTING."

"I'm just using blank shells I collected at the fishing club. They don't hurt anyone. It's just fun pretending to shoot at things."

My heart was banging so hard I was afraid it was going to give one more vicious thump and stop. It was sick of all the panicky alarms it had gone through helping me survive Max's exploits.

"WHAT IDIOT SOLD A 22- TO A 15-YEAR-OLD?"

"You don't have to shout at me."

"Yes, I do. Kids shouldn't have rifles. Guns should be locked up in gun cabinets. Not stashed under beds."

He looked at his bed with a furtive expression. I had used the expression as a classic example of a stupid place to hide something but he took it literally. I suddenly remembered the earlier reference to 'them'.

"The other gun's under the bed?"

"What other gun? I don't have another one."

At least Max felt the need to lie—he must have felt some qualms about the guns. Fortunately for me, he wasn't very good at lying.

"You said 'them' so I know there's at least one other one."

I just looked at him and tried not to blink. I could see his mind working. He may have no ability to put himself inside another person's mind but he did have a wonderful memory. From long experience he knew I usually discovered anything he wanted to keep hidden. He also knew I wouldn't give up if I thought something was wrong. His desire to share his other gun with me overrode his hope he could fake me out. He flopped to the floor, felt under his bed, pulled out a pellet gun and handed it to me barrel-first. I flinched and automatically pushed the end of the rifle to one side. I was so conditioned by my father to move the barrel so it wasn't aimed at me that I couldn't stop it. I even did it when I knew the gun was a toy. The kids thought this was funny. I didn't.

"Did Dan see these?" I assumed he would have taken them to the neighborhood's self-acclaimed gun expert and wannabe cowboy for approval. Max nodded.

"What did he say?"

Max beamed with pride. "He thought I got a good deal. The pellet gun isn't anything special but the 22- is. They don't make this model any more so it will just get more valuable each year."

Max had been obsessed with guns for as long as I could remember. One of his friends went shooting with his father. Max wanted to know why he and Pete couldn't do the same. This required buying a gun. When Max wanted to do something, he harangued me or Pete non-stop. Pete had been in the Navy in the Pacific Theater during the war so he knew how to shoot but had seen what guns did up close and had no desire to own one. But he empathized with Max so one Saturday, he came home from downtown Wilmette with a 22-caliber Beretta pistol and a gun trap. The working theory was that the trap would be set up in the basement and the boys could shoot under supervision.

The gun trap looked as though it had been designed by a mad welder who fabricated it in his basement. It was so heavy, the car bounced up when it was lifted out of the trunk. Painted matte black, it looked ominous. Constructed from thick steel plates cleverly placed so they formed a baffle that bounced the bullet back into a trap, it worked exactly as promised, assuming the shooter was able to aim the gun well enough to hit the opening. But this wasn't happening. After a ricocheted bullet almost took off my ear, I called a halt to using the cellar as a gun range with the promise we would bring the pistol and gun trap with us the following week when we took a camping trip out west.

It was a long week. I spent a lot of time keeping track of the gun. It sat next to the alarm clock beside my bed at night.

Finding a place where we could assume a deflected bullet wouldn't take out a fellow camper was poor. Every mile of the way, Max nagged. "Can't we stop? Can't we stop? Look. There's a field." He refused to concede some stranger might take umbrage at us using his side yard as a shooting gallery.

We finally found a place backed by a rise to prevent near misses from hitting an unseen person or cow. No dwellings, people or animals were visible. We were parked at the side of the road for an hour. Fortunately, few vehicles drove by. None stopped.

Linda and I read and Andrea colored three pages in her coloring book. I had noticed the color she used reflected the emotional level at the moment. This was a red day. Pete, Max and Seth wrangled. I looked up each time their voices rose. Max kept trying to grab the gun, allegedly to show Seth or Pete how to hold it—aim it—anything he could think of to get the gun in his hand. He quivered each time he had to give the gun to one of the others. It struck me that he was behaving like a serious alcoholic eyeing the only bottle of gin in the area.

Pete noted the intensity of Max's obsessive need to control the gun. When they came back to the car, he made a point of positioning the gun under his car seat in front of a strut so he was the only who could reach it. Max's fixation with the pistol grew with each road-side target practice. During the rest of the trip we made sure the gun was always in Pete's possession. When we got back to Wilmette, we both agreed we were better off with no guns in the house. Pete got rid of it without telling Max why he had done it or even that the gun was gone. I was the one who had to explain when I caught Max rummaging through Pete's drawers searching for what he thought of as *his* gun. Max was livid and assumed I had gotten rid of it without Pete's knowledge. When he told Pete what I had done, Pete just shrugged and looked disgusted. He never explained he was the one who had actually gotten rid of it.

Pete was furious when I told him that Max now had two rifles. He thought getting rid of the gun he bought had ended Max's obsession.

"Where the fuck did he get two guns?"

I told him.

"Where are they now?"

"I took them over to Dan's house. They're locked in his gun cabinet. How do you want to deal with them? We can't expect Dan to be responsible for them."

"They're going in the lake." His voice was hard.

"What do you mean—in the lake?"

"Just that."

"You can't just throw them away. You have to respect..."

"I can and I will."

Pete and I had an ethical split on the innate importance of respecting other people's property regardless of their age or relationship. He felt he had the right to control everything his children owned and pitched their belongings without a qualm. I had been fighting a running battle with him about this infringement of their rights ever since Linda was born. To my knowledge he hadn't disposed of any of my possessions yet.

"Look, disposing of his guns without some discussion of what he…"

He loomed over me and clenched his teeth so hard the muscles in his neck stood out. He was the only person I knew who could shout without raising his voice.

"THERE WILL BE NO GUNS IN *MY* HOUSE. GOT THAT? I DON'T WANT TO HEAR ANY OF YOUR FAIRNESS SHIT. THIS IS *MY* HOUSE AND *I* MAKE ALL THE RULES." He emphasized each word with his pointed index finger.

I instinctively cringed. His slashing forefinger was dangerously close to my nose. I wondered if he realized his hand was in the shape kids used to imitate a gun. It was a gesture he used frequently when he was angry.

When Pete calmed down I tried to explain I didn't want guns loose with what seemed to be a gun-obsessed teenager in the house but I felt that we should respect the guns' intrinsic worth and their value to Max. Aside from being legally questionable, throwing them into the lake was like smacking Max in the face. "Why don't we find a gun dealer, sell them and give Max the money."

Pete was too frustrated to listen to my point of view but was out of town for two weeks so nothing was done. Before he left, he said he had talked with Dan, who promised the guns would stay in the gun safe. I spent the two weeks researching where I could sell the guns without a legitimate bill of sale. A gun dealer in Wisconsin said he would buy the guns, no questions asked. He was clearly our best bet.

Pete came home on Friday. He still wanted to throw the guns into the lake until I reminded him Lake Michigan was a freshwater lake and relatively shallow. The guns would theoretically be usable no matter how long they were underwater. I didn't know any way to dump them far enough out in the lake so they couldn't be recovered. There were no bridges across the lake and no accessible piers extending far enough into the lake so the water was deep enough so guns couldn't be seen. I told him about the dealer in Wisconsin.

We drove up to the gun dealer later that morning. The dealer took one look at us and pegged us as desperate parents. We probably weren't the first gun dumpers.

The maximum amount he would give us was $25. Pete gave Max the money. Max was furious. At me. I suppose I should have been flattered he thought I had this much power over Pete.

Chapter 39

The family car was a gravel-dinged VW bus that looked like it had been strafed by a bunch of trigger-happy guerrillas. Boy Scout camp grounds all seemed to be down long gravel roads. It was not your typical Wilmette faux wood-paneled station-wagon. Linda insisted I park a block away when I dropped her off or picked her up.

Seth thought the ratty looking car was funny. He told his friends we got shot at a lot.

Max didn't seem to be aware the battered VW van was an anomaly in Wilmette.

Our second car was a red Triumph convertible. It was fun to drive, started in the sub-zero temperature readings so common in Illinois but had the traction of a toboggan on ice and a pitifully inadequate heater.

The north shore of Lake Michigan very rarely got the deep, lake effect snow that blanketed the south shore and Indiana. Our snowfall was rarely more than a few inches. Wilmette didn't salt the streets and was slow to plow so everyone had studded snow tires. We didn't put them on the Triumph because we never drove it in the winter.

Pete's and my relationship had deteriorated to the point where it didn't offer either of us much joy. I sometimes felt as if Pete and I spoke two different languages. I suspect he did too. Looking at our friends and neighbors, our marriage wasn't unusual. The 1960s was an era of significant change. The idea that women might have individual rights began to ferment and bubble under the surface but in staid Wilmette the weight of tradition prevailed. There were cracks here and there but the women's movement had no support to break through and be recognized, let alone supported.

Pete and I rarely had anything that would be considered an

outright argument. We didn't have enough face-to-face conversation time to squander it on controversy. The bulk of our communication was through cryptic notes left on the kitchen counter. Once I decided that I was going to try to make the marriage work and followed Pete to Chicago, I didn't know what else to do except to keep trying harder but I was losing heart. Pete dealt with our sagging relationship by suggesting we take a trip. It was expensive but cheaper than a divorce. So we went to Jamaica for a week. We come home suntanned, relatively rested and as ready to face another year of insanity as possible.

When we walked into the house, we knew something bad had happened. No one said hello. Eyes showed too much white and had difficulty focussing. Ann looked like someone in the middle of a scary nightmare. They were sitting around the dining room table with clean plates. It was after seven in the evening. They usually ate at five.

"What's wrong?"

Three voices answered. Max looked apprehensive and stayed mute. When we finally sorted through all the noise, we found out Max had gone joy riding in the Triumph and skidded off the ice covered road in the park by the lake. The police were called. They brought Max home. He was 15.

Ann lived in an area of Chicago south of the loop, a place where police were not considered friends. She was so horrified to see a policeman at the door she shrieked and dropped a large pitcher full of milk. She was still visibly upset. She said where she lived police didn't show up unless someone had been shot dead. And they didn't bring home underage kids driving on public streets without a license. They took the kids straight to jail. She said the Wilmette police brought the Triumph to the house when they realized there was no licensed driver available to pick it up. I wondered if they would have bothered if he had been driving the VW bus. I suspect that would have been towed to the pound.

Years later, Seth told me Max had been rolling the Triumph

down the alley before starting the motor and tooling around town ever since we had bought it. When I taught the children not to tattle on each other I should have added the caveat *unless it's Max*. But how was I to know ethical behavior was a waste when dealing with a person who didn't grasp the simple fact that other people had rights different from his? Fortunately, the car was unharmed. I traded it in for a new VW beetle two days later. A white one so it was highly visible.

That was our last vacation as an unfettered couple. The next year we drove to Florida for spring break with all four kids in tow. It was a change of scene but our marriage had deteriorated to the point where we needed what psychologists call quality time and lots of it if we were going to survive as anything more than parents of these four children.

We all enjoyed the sun after months of relentless cold and gray skies. But no one in their right mind would call the ten days a romantic vacation or even a simple respite.

Chapter 40

Halfway through Max's first year in high school, he was identified as a high IQ-low achiever pupil and put with a group of other boys with similar problems. The counselor who ran the group was a worldly, smart, empathetic man impossible to con. I met with the other group parents once a month. Pete came to the meetings if he was in town and not involved with Boy Scout functions.

The counselor took the boys on field trips and told me he could see why Max was often bored with school. "So far he's already been to every place in Chicago where I've taken the boys. He knows the museums and the subway better than I do. He ordered for us when we went to Chinatown, knows how to make Japanese fried rice and why it's different from the fried rice in Chinese restaurants. I don't know how to make either kind of rice, so I took him at his word."

"He's been eating both all his life," I told him. "Pete's art school room-mates taught us how to make the Japanese variety and close friends who grew up with Chinese parents taught us the other. I don't suppose Max told you he always picks out every bit of meat in the left-over Japanese-style fried rice and eats it. The meat's the best part so this drives the rest of us wild. We all end up yelling at him but nothing stops him."

"No, he skipped that part but I can picture it."

Only one parent at a time tended to show up at the meetings. I asked the counselor why. He looked amused. "You and your husband are the odd ones. The other parents are either separated or divorced. Not many marriages survive the constant wear of living with sons as difficult as Max. I'm surprised *you're* still married."

I accepted this as a compliment even though I knew he had it backward. We were still married largely *because* of Max. Pete and

I may not have been perfect parents or perfect mates for each other but we had one important attribute in common that glued us together. We knew we were the best parents Max was ever going to get.

Chapter 41

Linda was a sophomore when Max started high school. She was tall, model thin and gorgeous. Junior and senior boys had started hitting on her the first week of her freshman year. We had been warned by the parents of two pretty girls who had survived New Trier High School that these boys would woo Linda, do their best to con her into sex then drop her, smear her reputation and go after the next naive pretty girl. So we told her she was not going to date until she was 16 and had the confidence to handle herself no matter what came up. This sounds draconian in 2007 when casual sex is accepted but it made sense in 1966 when being labeled promiscuous in high school could ruin the next four years. By the time she graduated from junior high, she had already come to the conclusion that she didn't want to hang out with what she called the cool girls. They were already dating, some were sexually active and their parents all belonged to the club with the most cachet in the area.

Linda was great at understanding social mores. She knew we were offbeat for the wealthy suburb. Her father was a scout master. Her mother did artwork for money, repaired things around the house and mowed the lawn instead of playing bridge, and wouldn't buy her an expensive authentic Scottish kilt regardless of how many girls had one. Her brother was weird. Only a hippie would drive the family cars. And most damning of all, her parents would not consider joining the exclusive club even if they were asked. She knew neither Pete nor I had any interest in spending time with people who wouldn't welcome all of our varied friends.

A pragmatic realist, Linda saw us as so out of tune with Wilmette norms she decided she might as well hang out with a group of girls who didn't worry about boys and had fun. She became a Mariner Scout, a rare but quite viable section of senior

Girl Scouts. This was a great choice in Wilmette. Mariner Scouts crewed on the boats in the Wilmette Yacht Basin and spent two summer vacations as crew on the topsail schooner Shenandoah sailing the waters off Cape Cod.

We had a family game we often played at get-togethers with Wing and Pearl and their family. We called it Killer Solitaire. Each player had their own deck and the rules of play were the same as usual except that the aces were put in the center and played on by everyone. It was intense, extremely competitive, merciless and fun. There was a great deal of shrieking and laughing. Everyone was equal. Max rarely played. He said later, he couldn't stop himself from stacking the cards the way he would have if he were playing by himself so he never won. Pete didn't play either.

As soon as one of the children displayed an interest, they were taught how to play Solitaire. When they were fast enough so they didn't slow the game, they were asked to join in. It was an odd but important rite of passage. Linda loved the game. When she came home from school, she often got out a couple of decks and we played solitaire while she told me what had gone on at school. It was usually the best part of my day.

Linda got her driver's license shortly after she turned 16. As soon as Pete and I were comfortable with her behind the wheel, she was allowed to take the car to school on those occasions when she had a dentist or doctor's appointment and she was eventually allowed to have friends in the car.

The downside of this was Max. He shoved his way into the car regardless of where she was going then criticized her driving and insisted on tagging along when she was going to the mall or a movie with friends. Max obviously counted on her not tattling on him.

Max got a learner's permit to drive as soon as this was possible and passed his driver's test the day after he turned 16. He was incensed when I wouldn't just hand over the car keys and let him roll.

"I told you before you got your permit either your dad or I would let you drive whenever possible but one of us was going to be in the car with you until we were comfortable with the way you drove."

"That's not fair. The State of Illinois thinks I'm qualified. Who are you to decide I have to be baby-sat when I drive?"

"The car's owners."

After Max got his license, he drove Linda wild when she was given the car. He waited until she had unlocked the car, twisted her arm until she had to drop the keys, shoved her out of the way and slid into the driver's seat. She found this particularly infuriating if she was going somewhere with friends because Max wouldn't let anyone else talk without butting in. Max didn't realize Linda could only be pushed so far. He snatched the keys one time too many. Linda stood in the middle of the street and screamed with frustration. Her scream was still glass-shattering. A neighbor ran across the street expecting bloodshed. Linda told him what Max had done. Embarrassed, Max gave her the keys and got out of the car. This was far more effective than anything I could have done.

The neighbor had six somewhat eccentric kids so he wasn't fazed. He just laughed and said, "That's some scream."

Chapter 42

Max got a job pumping gas at a downtown station. The first few times I gave him the car to drive to and from work, he showed up back home exactly when he was expected. Then he was a few minutes later than normal. In most towns, this wouldn't have been an issue as long as he wasn't too late getting home, but in Wilmette it was looking for trouble.

Wilmette had a curfew. This gave any kid under 18 a great way to harass parents. They had to be with a parent or have a job with a permission slip signed by the parents and their employer to stay out after 10 o'clock on school nights and 11 o'clock on weekends. Max was picked up regularly. I told him he was going to have to walk home on the nights I couldn't fetch him. He could no longer take the car. I decided he was less likely to get into serious trouble if he was walking. He had a job that theoretically ended at 9 o'clock so the permission slip wouldn't work.

I knew Max could get the ten blocks from the gas station to the house unseen if that was what he wanted to do. But he practically walked down the middle of the street so no patrolling police officer could miss him.

Wilmette was a bad town to live in with an angry passive/aggressive child. And Max seemed to become angrier every day. He had fought with Seth, pounding him mercilessly ever since Seth started school. I don't think a week went by without me having to yank them apart. When they were young, Seth resorted to biting to try to even the bitter contest. Fearful Seth would bite off a finger, part of an ear, or gouge out an eye; I ended up disciplining both boys. This was clearly unfair. Seth never started the fights. He ended up even more convinced Max got preferential treatment. Unfortunately, children quantify parental love by the relative time spent with other siblings. Eventually, Seth got big enough to pummel Max with enough force to make fist fights too painful. So Max directed his anger at me. I was always there, a constant in his increasingly chaotic life. I was the disciplinarian, the obvious bad guy.

It isn't easy being 16 years old. It was doubly frustrating for Max because he didn't understand why people wouldn't let him run his own life exactly the way he wanted. I told him he was putting himself in positions where he dared authority figures to get in his face. Linda was occasionally out after curfew. No one ever bothered her because she made an effort to fade into the woodwork. Even his friend Joe, who completely ignored the curfew, was never challenged for much the same reason.

I finally told Max he had to quit the job. I'd had it with lectures from police officers each time I picked him up at the police station. I felt like my life was being squashed between Max's incomprehensible, flagrant misbehavior and the disapproval of police and teachers. They couldn't reach him, so they attacked me.

Max was seeing a very good psychologist once a week. He enjoyed their sessions. The man was intelligent, had a good sense of the ridiculous, had seen this self-destructive behavior before, but like the counselor who ran the high IQ-low achiever group, he had no idea how to change Max's behavior or even what prompted it.

He confirmed my sense that Max's antics were significantly more serious than normal teenage angst. Clearly brilliant, Max was utterly unable to comprehend what was going on in other people's minds. He could relate cause and effect after it happened but not why he kept being hassled when he wasn't doing anything he considered wrong. He had an incredible memory, he could relate in painful detail every incident where he had gotten into trouble but he couldn't grasp why he had to follow what seemed to him to be arbitrary rules. He got a ticket for driving another boy's car at midnight. It was too long after curfew for a reprimand. A parent had to accompany him to court. Pete and I both went. Pete didn't want to be there. I didn't either so I was grateful for his presence. When Max was called in front of the judge, Pete and I walked with him to the front of the courtroom. Pete planted himself in front of the judge with his arms across his chest. He was tall. I was short and not intimidating to anyone except three or four-year-olds. Max was still small for his age. Next to his father he looked even smaller. I could see he was trying to mimic his father's challenging stance. It was oddly touching.

The judge leaned forward, his elbows resting on the polished walnut dais, his chin cupped in one hand. After the formality of establishing identity, he read the charge and asked Max why he was driving someone else's car after curfew.

Max pulled himself up to his full height and said, "I was the only one in the car not under the influence of tetrahydro-cannabinol."

The judge's eyebrows shifted upward, furrowing his brow. He nodded. "I see. That changes things. That wasn't in the police report."

I knew what this was. It wasn't easy keeping a saccharine, mealy-mouthed expression but I'd had a lot of practice dealing with Max's fall-out. Pete looked blank. He had no clue what Max had just said. Math and science were his brother's expertise. Family lore still had the brother labeled as the smart one. He had been dead for 20 years now but Pete still felt his brother's shadow and worked hard to be his opposite so he never read science articles.

The judge turned to Pete. "That didn't mean anything to you, did it?"

Pete shook his head and shrugged. "No. Should it?"

"I assume you're familiar with marijuana.
Tetrahydrocannabinol is the active ingredient."

Pete's shoulders tightened. He shook his head. *He* got the lecture this time. He didn't like it. The judge ignored me. I was happy to be considered unimportant. When the case was dismissed, Pete turned and stalked out of the room, shaking his head.

In the car, he kept muttering that he couldn't believe Max got out of a traffic ticket by admitting to a felony. I couldn't blame him for feeling frustrated.

When his understandable irritation shifted to ridicule of Max, I had to stop him but didn't know how without saying something. I never contradicted him in front of the kids. Max couldn't see my hand. I reached over and touched Pete's arm. He yanked his arm away as though I were jabbing him with a blowtorch and gave me a venomous glance but was quiet.

Like any merger, marriage has what I think of as a point system. Each partner in a marriage has expectations. If these mesh with the spouse's expectations, the points stay equally high. Pete and I were bilaterally close to rock bottom. We still meshed on curiosity and taste. We used to agree on wit. He had what was described as rapier wit. Like the description, it was fast and could cut but it was often very funny.

When I was the butt of Pete's wit I could protest but I usually ended up laughing. I stopped laughing when the kids were ridiculed. They cared too much. Every time I protested on their behalf, I lost points. But nothing I said stopped him doing it.

Max described the kids' reaction to Pete's sharp tongue.

"When Dad makes fun of me, I hurt as though he just stuck a knife in my chest. I'm mad at myself for laughing but I can't stop because it's so funny."

Chapter 43

"GET YOUR HANDS OFF ME." Max was shrieking. I heard Pete's voice but couldn't figure out what he had said. They were in the family room watching TV.

I was in the living room reading to Andrea. I stood up but was knocked back in the chair as Max hurtled through the living room. His face was bright red. He looked furious and close to tears. Pete followed close behind. He looked stunned. Max yanked open the front door and ran out. It was mid-February, hovering around 20 degrees – that's 12 degrees below freezing – and Max was barefoot.

Pete reached for Max's arm. "For God's sake, put some shoes on."

Max yanked his arm away and came close to falling down the steps. "GET YOUR FUCKING HANDS OFF ME. I HATE YOU. YOU'RE NEVER GOING TO TOUCH ME AGAIN."

He leaped down the steps and ran down the street shrieking, "SHIT-FUCK, SHIT-FUCK, SHIT-FUCK," at the top of his lungs. Still shrieking, "SHIT-FUCK," his voice diminished and finally faded in the distance.

I was shivering. "Should I go after him?"

"No. Give him a chance to cool off. He's barefoot. He won't go far." Pete watched him until he disappeared, then closed the door.

Andrea came over and wrapped her arms around my legs and clung to me as though she wanted to merge with the relative safety of my body. I picked her up and hugged her. She pressed her head and shoulders against me, clutched me with her left arm and stuck her right thumb in her mouth. Five years old and ready to be independent by now, Max's out of control behavior and animosity toward her kept thwarting her. He made the house feel like a dangerous place to all of us. I was often tense and uneasy when he was at home. I know I transmitted this to Andrea.

I turned to Pete. "What happened?"

"Damned if I know." He shook his head and went back to the TV.

I tried to clean the kitchen but kept picking up things and putting them down. The doors to the basement playroom were locked. I ran down, unlocked them and left the light on so Max could slip in. I grabbed my coat and ran back to the garage and made sure it was unlocked. I was chilled to the bone in a down coat. How far could Max go barefoot and without a coat without serious frostbite? We were a block from a large church. Their door would still be unlocked. The church was heated. I hoped he had the sense to go inside. But I doubted it. He might have to explain why he was running around in the bitter cold without shoes or a coat. Everyone jumped when the phone rang. I answered it. With no greeting or preamble, Max said, "Can I talk to Seth?"

"Sure." I handed the phone to Seth. Pete and Andrea hovered next to me. I heard Linda walk out into the upstairs hall and stand next to the rail to listen.

After Seth's hello, I heard Max talking. Seth said, "Just a minute. I have to get a paper and pencil."

I grabbed one out of the drawer and handed it to him. He wrote what looked like a list, said, "Okay," and hung up.

He turned to Pete and me, hunched his shoulders, extended his hands in a classic imploring gesture and said, "What am I supposed to do now? Max made me promise I wouldn't tell you where he is but he wants me to bring a bunch of stuff to Joe's house."

Seth was thirteen. Amazed at the convoluted way Max's mind worked, I laughed with relief. "Did he say how he wanted you to get the stuff there?"

"I didn't ask. He knows I don't have a driver's license. Joe's house is farther away than my school. I'm not going to walk that far."

Seth read off the items from the list. I collected them and packed them in a duffel bag. Linda stayed with Andrea. Pete drove the three of us over to Joe's house. It was almost a mile away. We parked half a block from the house to perpetuate the myth Seth could summon a magic carpet to transport him across town. When Seth got back in the car, he said, "He didn't ask who drove me. He just took the duffel bag and closed the door. He probably thinks I drove myself. That's what he would do."

Max came home after school at the usual time the next day and stayed and ate dinner with the other kids. I assumed he was home to stay. When I asked why he ran out of the house in the first place, he just shrugged. As soon as he finished eating, he went up to his room. A little later, I heard a car drive up, followed by the bounding thuds of Max's feet running down the stairs. Then the front door was yanked open and slammed shut. It was a solid house but I could feel the reverberations from the slammed door through the kitchen floor. Later that evening, I got a call from the police. They wanted me to collect Max at the police station. Fortunately, Linda was home to watch Andrea. The man at the front desk at the police station looked me over with an unusually cold eye when I asked him where I would find Max. He pointed to the area where someone was screaming, "Fuck, fuck, fuck." I suddenly felt sick. It was Max. The desire to walk back out the door was overwhelming. I was thoroughly sick of being a responsible parent.

Probably because my mother was so unpredictable in her craziness, I worked hard to learn how to be invisible. Any notice was a potential threat. A friend once commented I'd perfected the opposite of the dramatic entrance. Max's never-ending defiance of all forms of normal behavior focussed constant, usually critical attention on me. I found this a form of torture. At this moment I wanted to disown this angry, impossible child who

187

blighted my life but it would have been like walking away from a bloody car crash. I tried hard to look like the caring parent I was, thanked the desk officer and walked back to the source of the noise.

Max was standing in the merciless glare of a fluorescent ceiling fixture. His eyes were vivid red. His repeated profanity was slurred but unmistakable. He was engulfed in a marijuana fog I could smell ten feet away. It looked as though he was trying to get his ID out of his wallet. He ignored me when I said, "Knock it off with the language, Max."

It wasn't the "I'm not going to acknowledge you" attitude all kids master early on. It was as though I really didn't exist. Unfortunately, the three uniformed officers standing around him didn't share Max's belief I wasn't in the room. They turned and looked at me with disgust. It was a look I had seen often from people who assumed I had the power to control his behavior and chose not to. I felt a great desire to pound all their heads together and scream. My face must have reflected this spasm of temper because the officer who appeared to be in charge frowned at me.

I took a deep, slow breath, willed my voice to be calm and reasonable and addressed the frowning man. "What's the charge, Officer?" I knew it wasn't smoking dope. Max's school counselor had told me the only pot-related arrests in Wilmette were for dealing. This was the land of high-priced lawyers. The police had arrested people in good faith and been burned too many times. And he wasn't picked up for curfew violation, it was just nine o'clock.

"You're the mother?" I nodded. "Your boy looked like he might be in trouble. We just wanted to make sure he got home okay."

"Thank you." I didn't tell them I wasn't sure if he was living at his home at the moment. Sometimes it was just too complicated to explain Max logic. Each "fuck" spewing from Max's mouth earned me a further glance of contempt from the officers. They finally released him into my custody. I thanked them and followed Max's weaving figure out to the street. He lunged off in the opposite direction from my car. "You might consider going in the same direction I do in case someone's looking out the window." My voice was sarcastic. I had experienced more than my fill of Max's anti-social behavior in the last 24 hours. I was sick of kindness and consideration for Max's feelings. No one gave a damn about my feelings. Why couldn't someone be kind to me for a change?

"Fuck them. I'm not going home with you as long as Dad lives there. I don't care about those pigs."

I felt helpless fury watching him stagger off. Damn it. I hated this life I was leading. Why did everyone assume *I* had taught Max to behave in a way I would never condone? I was so law abiding I even stopped at red lights if there were no cars visible for ten miles in any direction. Because of Max I had spent more time in police stations than an inept bank robber. When he turned the corner, I had the fleeting wish he would just keep walking.

At that moment I would have given years of my life to be free of this impossible boy. I decided this had to be the low point of life with Max.

Max and Joe both showed up at our house after school the next day. They looked normal. They had obviously had more sleep than I did.

Max said, "What's for supper?" This was pretty much his normal opening conversational gambit when he came home from school. He was clearly taking lessons from his father. I was so used to hearing it in some form or another I just answered with little thought. But I was tired and feeling crabby. It was hard to muster up any warm, fuzzy, nurturing feelings.

"Chicken pot pie." I nodded at Joe and faced Max with my hands propped on my hips, effectively blocking his path through the kitchen.

"So what was last night's drama all about?"

Max elbowed me aside and started up the stairs to his room. "Nothing you would understand."

I moved back so Joe could follow then raised my voice so Max could hear me as he clanged up the metal stairs to his room. "Try me. You'd be surprised at what I can grasp." But he didn't answer.

The other children were eating by the time Max and Joe came back down. Linda rolled her eyes. Her voice sarcastic, she said, "After your dramatic departure a couple days ago, I kind of hoped you were never planning to darken our door again."

Joe looked embarrassed but Max's face didn't change. I'm not sure he even registered her taunt. Max couldn't multi-task. He concentrated on what was most immediately relevant. On this bitter cold winter afternoon, that was eating. I doubted if Joe's mother had packed Max a lunch.

When I came back downstairs after giving Andrea her bath, Max and Joe were gone. My car was still in the driveway. Joe's car was gone. I assumed they had gone to his house. I don't think there's a guide for proper manners when your teenage kid has sort of run away and you know where he is and have just fed him and his run-away host. I decided I better check with Joe's mother to find out how she felt about Max staying in her house.

Joe answered when I called. He said his mother and father were out.

"I just wanted to be sure they don't mind having Max underfoot."

Joe made no audible sound, yet I had the odd sensation I was hearing him think. He finally said, "They like Max. He talks to them." There was another brief silence, then he said. "They're research chemists." I decided that was as good an answer as I would get so I thanked him and hung up.

The two boys showed up, eating like starving stevedores for the next two days. The following day Max arrived alone. He still wouldn't talk about what had triggered his abrupt departure earlier in the week.

When Pete got home they both acted as though nothing had ever happened. As far as I was able to determine, they didn't discuss the incident. I never knew if the trigger that sent Max careening into the bitter cold barefoot had been so trivial that neither of them could remember it or so terrible that neither of them was willing to broach it again.

I asked Pete again if he could recall what had caused the whole scene. He just looked at me with a blank expression on his face and went back to reading his paper without comment or any change of expression. Max's response had been similar. The rude way they dismissed me was irritating but I was used to it. It was something my father had always done when a date came for me. Pete, Max and my dad were so similar in their ability to ignore anything they didn't want to acknowledge, it worried me. If my father was an example of selective rudeness, we were in for a rough time.

Linda was in the process of picking a college. Unlike the mothers of most of her friends, I didn't have to nag her to send for brochures or get recommendations and transcripts. She obviously couldn't wait to get away. Her main criterion was that the school be as far away from Wilmette as possible. She said, "I'm going to find a school in another part of the country. And I'm never coming home until Max leaves. He ruins everything for me."

I cut in. "I know he hassles you about the car but..."

"Hassles! *Hassles!* He almost broke my arm yesterday when I wouldn't give him the car keys. You said *I* could drive to Sally's house after work. But he snatched the keys and bent my wrist when I wouldn't let go."

"I thought you *did* go to Sally's house."

"Yeah. But my stupid brother drove me there. We were going to go to the mall and Max wouldn't drive us there unless we let him come with us. Then he drove us crazy talking about motor-cycles. He can't get it through his head we don't care about motorcycles."

"What do your friends say when he pulls stuff like this?"

"They're nice about it. They all have brothers and sisters who give them a hard time."

"Are any of their siblings like Max?"

"Are you kidding? No one's as bizarre as Max. At least they believe me when I say what a nightmare he is to live with. Did you ever try to explain Max to a stranger? It's like trying to explain a marauding water buffalo to someone who has never seen an animal larger than a rabbit."

Chapter 44

I was sitting at the drawing board in my studio on the third floor across from Max's bedroom finishing the visuals for a sales meeting at a large medical supply company. I had resigned my teaching job at the Art Institute of Chicago three years earlier but I had wanted to keep Ann two days a week. Driven by a Puritan streak, I did enough freelance artwork to pay her and pay for the psychologist Max was still seeing.

The roar of a motorcycle down in the alley drew me to the window of Max's room. He and another boy were admiring the boy's motorcycle. Nothing unusual. I went back to my drawing board.

Max's interest in motorcycles hadn't abated. He still had days when he followed me around the kitchen talking about motor-cycles as I made supper. Or guns. He didn't seem to care that I had no clue what he was talking about. Anyone other than Max would have realized I had no interest in either subject. I was polite because I could see both topics were important to him so I nodded a lot and made appropriate noises. I often suggested he find someone who knew what he was saying and could give him feedback but I might as well have been talking to myself.

When I went downstairs, I was surprised to find Max alone. I didn't hear the motorcycle leaving. That's because it didn't. Max had just bought it. I wasn't really surprised. I checked to be sure he had all the correct paperwork then I sat next to him and looked him in the eye. "Let me warn you of one thing, Max. If you ever get picked up for *any* traffic violation or smoke dope and ride your bike, I will get rid of it if I have to take it apart and distribute the pieces in trash cans all over town."

"That's not fair." He watched me, clearly trying to figure out why I would say such a thing. He obviously failed at this because he made another try at faking me out. "You won't know if I smoke dope."

I just looked at him. "You've got to be kidding. I have a great sense of smell. I can smell pot the minute you walk in the door."

"How come you don't say anything?"

"I do. Frequently. You just tune me out."

He was looking worried. "You couldn't take the bike apart. You don't have the right tools."

"Max, I can take anything apart." I sounded as nasty as I felt. "If I can't find the right tools, there's always the sledgehammer. I'm good with a sledgehammer."

I could see he believed me now. He looked horrified.

I felt like a Borgia but surviving Max was a no-holds-barred kind of life.

Dan, our local gun and motorcycle expert, took Max over to the park and watched him ride the bike. Dan owned three of them and still had all his body parts. I decided that qualified him as an expert. He said Max rode it well. He sounded surprised. Max tended to be ungainly but the bike seemed to smooth out his tendency to flail his arms.

We were scheduled to leave for Florida in two weeks. We had traded in the VW bus and now had a large Oldsmobile station wagon with a trailer hitch. No trailer: Pete needed the hitch to haul canoes for Boy Scouts. Max wanted to bring the motorcycle to Florida. He checked out motorcycle carriers we could haul. Pete vetoed this. Pete had to go to New York the day before we were to leave. He said he would fly down and meet us in Fort Lauderdale. I was not looking forward to driving for three days but I was keen to get away.

I heard the motorcycle early the next morning. It was still dark. The clock radio read 5:13. Weird. Why would Max go anywhere now? We were planning to leave as soon as rush hour was over. I went down to make coffee and found a note on the counter.

DEAR MOM
I AM RIDING THE BIKE TO FLORIDA. LEE IS GOING WITH
ME. HE IS PAYING FOR GAS AND FOOD. I TOOK A BAG
OF COOKIES AND MADE 4 SANDWICHES. WE HAVE
SLEEPING BAGS. HIS PARENTS SAID IT'S OKAY. THEY
WENT TO OHIO. DON'T WORRY. I WILL BE CAREFUL.
LOVE MAX.

I read and re-read the note, hoping it would look different if I just read it to death. I wanted to call Lee's parents to find out if they were really in Ohio only to find their phone was unlisted. I didn't know where they lived. I couldn't drive to their house and hope Lee slept late so I could intercept them. My panic was kept in check by the grim stoicism I had acquired to survive Max. I knew there was nothing I could do other than have the police pick them up. And I was sure this was a potentially bad idea. I didn't know what Max would do if he was pulled over. I may have been mentally maligning him but maybe not. So far, he had managed to go beyond my direst imaginings. I was afraid he might decide to go off road and cut across a field rather than pull over.

I called Pete at his hotel in New York. He mulled it over.

"Don't call the cops. I know you hate motorcycles. But this is how boys grow up. I'm glad he had the sense to bring another kid with him. How big is he?"

"What difference does Lee's size make?"

"If he's bigger than Max, they're less likely to be hassled."

"He's no bruiser but he *is* bigger than Max." I didn't tell him the boy looked like a wimp and didn't seem to understand the body shifts needed when riding on a two-wheeled vehicle. Max had told me Lee's parents wouldn't buy him a bike when he was younger because they were afraid he would get hurt. I wondered if they really knew how he was getting to Florida. I hoped they weren't the kind of people who liked to sue.

The trip with only three kids was peaceful except for a short, violent bout of food poisoning from a hamburger Seth ate. I stopped at a hardware store and bought a bucket, offered him sympathy but kept driving. He felt fine the next day. By then it was warm and we stopped at every Stuckey's we passed until we had our fill of peanut brittle. This was a rite of passage when we got below the Mason-Dixon Line.

Max arrived in Fort Lauderdale about seven hours after we did. He looked tired and triumphant. His trip home was less fortunate. The bike broke down south of Chicago. Max made an arrangement with a service station to leave his bike there for a fee. He and Lee hitched rides home. Max wanted Pete or me to rent a motorcycle carrier and drive him to the gas station where he had left his bike. Pete was unavailable. All his spare time was taken up with Boy Scouts. I refused. There were practical reasons. It would have been a long, tedious drive with a trailer attached to the car and would have required dragging Andrea and Seth with me. We had just spent three days cooped up in the car. This time Max would be with us. The dynamics were bad when these three got together. If there had been a good reason to make the effort, I would have done it and tried to make the best of it. But this was in the realm of favors and Max had used up far more than his quota of these long ago. I didn't even feel guilty.

Max added this to the long list of ways I had failed him. His mental list of the ways everyone in the family had wronged him was long and detailed but hopelessly skewed. It completely disregarded the idea any of us might have had any rights or even opinions of our own.

As Pete had predicted, the motorcycle trip bolstered Max's confidence. Now he didn't feel guilty when he drove off to pick up a friend at midnight. There was an element of calculation in this. He always waited until I had picked up Pete from the station, served him dinner and he had gone to bed. Max knew I would only waken Pete if there were a life-threatening emergency.

The Oldsmobile was currently our only car. In Wilmette a high end station wagon was close to invisible. I rarely heard Max leave but I often heard him come home. I protested. He looked at me with opaque eyes and brushed past me. I hid the keys. The first time I was distracted and left the keys on the counter, he took them and had a duplicate set made.

Eventually a cop who had dealt with Max before noticed him when he was stopped at a traffic light and he was hauled in. It was long after curfew. The police called me. I was supposed to pick him up.

"It'll take me a while. The car he was driving is the only one we have now. I'll have to walk."

"You only have one car?" He sounded dumbfounded. "Just a sec." I heard a second voice suggesting I ask a neighbor to drive me. The officer relayed this to me.

"Not at 1:30 in the morning. I'm not going to drag anyone out of bed at this hour. I'll walk. I should be there within the hour."

"Uh. Stay put. We'll bring Max and the car home."

This time Max was cited. Pete said he had no stomach for another lecture. I went to court with Max. It was a different judge. As usual, he wanted to know why I couldn't control my son and centered much of his stern lecture on me. He kept telling me I should just tell Max "No" and punish him when he misbehaved.

Recently turned 17 and full of himself, Max looked so indifferent he verged on rude but, out of habit, his voice was polite and he called the judge "sir."

I wanted to say, see, see, that's what *I* did. Give me *some* credit. How many 16-year old boys call you sir? Do you have any idea how many times I lined up my kids and drilled good manners into them? They even know what to do if they meet the Queen of England, for God's sake. But I didn't say anything. I just nodded and looked as polite as I could while stifling the desire to scream at every person who was making my life so miserable, starting with Max.

The judge segued into a soliloquy about the damage broken homes were inflicting on society. Suddenly realizing where he was going with this, I said, "Max doesn't come from a broken home. His father and I are still married."

He shook his head and frowned. I didn't think he liked being wrong when he was on his bandwagon. "Why isn't he here then?"

"He said he didn't want to listen to another lecture." This was probably the wrong thing to say but I was sick of being put in the position of defending everyone else's reputation. I clamped my mouth shut. I was too drained by this futile song and dance to trust myself. Nothing I did or said had any affect on Max. As his headmaster had said years earlier, he didn't get it. Why couldn't anyone understand this?

The judge blinked and stared at me. Then he said, "I better not see him in *my* court again."

Chapter 45

Halfway through the first semester in his junior year, Max's math teacher told him he would get a failing grade unless he did every homework assignment for the entire semester. Max protested. He aced all the tests, why did he have to turn in the homework? He had his own way of learning.

It was first grade all over again. Only this time, I sided with the teacher. With math, the correct answer could be less important than the method of reaching it.

Max finally spent a long evening methodically doing every homework assignment. In order to expedite this tortuous job he used one of his father's large bond paper pads, carefully numbering and drawing neat boxes around each day's work. He showed me the resulting sheets with obvious pride. I was pleased and told him so. He then rolled them and submitted them to the teacher.

The teacher wouldn't even look at the work. He told Max he had to redo it on individual sheets of paper. Max reacted as though the man had just slapped him in the face. He ripped the large sheet into bits, dropped these into the wastepaper basket and stalked to his assigned seat.

I was sick when I heard this. What kind of a teacher would be so destructive with a brilliant kid who loved math and showed he was willing to do the scut work in order to learn more? I talked with his counselor. He was equally disgusted with the teacher but couldn't do anything to change the outcome. He said he was worried about Max. High IQ-low achievers can thrive if they make it to the right college. If they don't, they can become so angry with the world they aren't fit to do anything and end up on the street.

He shook his head. "Max's too naive and vulnerable to survive there. He worries me when he rants about running away from home and becoming a hippie. That can be an ugly world."

The New Trier school district had a rigid dress code. In a town with a major yacht basin that hosted Olympic races, it was full of world class yachts and people in boat shoes without socks but for some reason the school insisted socks had to be worn at all times on the school's premises.

This made Max's contest with his teacher simple. He stopped wearing socks. He had them on when he left the house and when he entered the school building but they magically disappeared before he showed up for his math class. He was at war with the teacher. I don't think he cared if he won. Each time Max walked into the class, the teacher made him leave the room until he had missed enough classes to be kicked out of the class. There were no adults in this contest.

Max was clearly depressed. He talked constantly about running away. I empathized with him. He had no successes to help him through the failures. Each time I heard the sound of the car coming back from one of his late night forays, I relaxed enough to sleep for a few hours. Inevitably Max was picked up and cited again. I took him to court. We were lucky enough to get a judge who didn't know him so we just got the lecture. I got the impression the judges didn't like the curfew any more than the kids did. It had to be wearing sitting there day after day telling sulky kids the same thing. At least Max called the judge "sir." The next time he was cited I figured our luck was bound to run out. I lost a lot of points but insisted Pete come with us.

We got the ultimatum judge. He informed us we were doing a terrible job of parenting. If Max appeared in front of him again, he would be made a ward of the court and removed from our household.

We were too shocked to talk on the drive home. Pete didn't go to work. He paced back and forth, turning the TV on and off repeatedly. He finally suggested that we sell the house and move to Florida where, as he said, we always had a good time. We could scale down our lifestyle and work less and he could spend more time with Max. His IQ would make Max eligible for Nova High School. The change of school sounded good. Nova had been written up recently and did seem better suited to Max's learning style. I felt dread at any move but anything seemed better than the current situation. Having Max named a ward of the court would put him in a foster home. That would be tantamount to throwing him to a pack of wolves.

Pete resigned from his job and the Boy Scouts. I was surprised to see he didn't seem to regret either loss. I was under the impression both were important to him.

Six weeks before we were due to move, he opened his eyes one morning and said, "Let's go to Russia."

"Why Russia?"

"I've always wanted to go there. It'll be a learning experience for the kids."

The house sold fast. Two weeks before our moving day, Pete and I came home from an early evening farewell party. Linda had a date and Seth had gone to a movie with a friend. We had Andrea with us.

Max was going through a bout of pyromania. So far he had stuck to candles. I stopped buying them but had to keep a few short candles for the times when high winds knocked over trees and we lost power.

The distinctive odor of burnt wood and candle wax greeted us when we opened the front door. Max had gone out leaving a candle stuck on the sill of the large double-paned window in the kitchen. The fire had consumed the wick and instead of guttering out, had set the pool of melted wax on fire, burnt through the window sill and cracked the four foot by five foot, one quarter inch thick inner glass pane. I tried to be grateful the outer pane was still whole but it was a struggle. We couldn't find anyone to replace the glass in time for the move so we ended up doing it ourselves. I was left with a monster pane of thick glass. The trash firm in Wilmette wouldn't take it.

I finally laid an old canvas drop cloth on the cement in front of the garage, put the pane of glass on it, covered this with another drop cloth and whaled at it with my largest sledge-hammer. It was surprisingly hard to smash that much extra thick glass into pieces small enough to be hidden in trash but the job had its good points. It got rid of a lot of free-floating aggression.

If casting spells were possible, a number of people in the area would have been flinching. Whacking large pieces of thick glass with a ten-pound sledgehammer had to carry a stronger curse than sticking pins into a wax figure.

Chapter 46

Two months later we were on a BOAC flight on our way to London. It was late June. We would be in England and Russia close enough to the summer solstice to enjoy the long midsummer evenings. The plane swung out over the ocean and flew parallel to the East Coast for the first hour or so. The scene to the left of the plane was the sort of over-the-top view of raw nature 3D theater-goers loved. An enormous weather front was moving in from the west. Back-lit by the sun, the roiling, dark gray clouds spewed arced flashes of lightning that filled the western sky for the first hour or so of the flight from Miami International Airport. Up as high as we were, the bank of angry clouds appeared to stop at the coast. In front of us and to the east the sky was clear. Bright stars began to appear.

It was a great send-off. I hoped it was a portent of a change in our luck. I loved to fly. After two hectic months of constant motion, I could finally relax and enjoy myself.

The Iron Curtain was showing signs of cracking but was still very much in place. We were going to Russia but had gotten caught in a posturing standoff between our state department and the Kremlin. We had planned to start in Russia and made all the plane and hotel reservations but because of a dust-up between a couple of people in the American embassy in Moscow, the Russians punished us by changing all the reservations in Russia. Fortunately, this sort of thing happened often enough so our State Department helped us rearrange the rest of the trip. London was our first stop, Russia our second, Denmark the third and Spain last. We would be traveling for five weeks.

This was the first time the kids had been to Europe. I was glad we started in England. They loved it. It was a great non-threatening transition. They had seen Mexico, Canada and most of the United States and felt well-traveled but from the minute we boarded the Aeroflot Ilyushin Jet at Heathrow Airport for the flight to Leningrad, they were wide-eyed. They had spent a lot of time in airplanes and were used to the constantly refurbished interiors standard on American planes. The Ilyushin jet was sleek and elegant from the outside but had clearly never been refurbished on the inside. The kids stared at the broken tables in front of them and the stained and frayed seats. They were intrigued when the flight attendant brought us all small glasses of champagne, holding them with a finger stuck in each glass rather than on a pristine tray. Then they were disconcerted when the flight attendant gave champagne to seven-year-old Andrea and was clearly put-out when I refused it and asked if they had juice. The crabby flight attendant brought a glass of apple juice and plunked it down on Andrea's tray with such force half of it splashed out of the glass.

A group of students were going to a Russian language institute near Leningrad. One student spotted Max. A boy I had never seen before yelled, "Hey Max." It was a boy who had been in a number of Max's classes at New Trier High School. The two boys chatted with the relief of people finding the familiar in the midst of chaos.

On landing, we were met by the Intourist representative assigned to us. We had been warned by our own state department that we would be watched at all times. This would normally have struck us as funny but we worried what they would make of Max. He had been allowing his thick hair to grow during the last semester in New Trier. By the time we were ready to leave for Europe, it was well below his ears and a definite anti-establishment statement. We had insisted he have it cut. I sympathized with him when he refused. I agreed it was his hair. I said if he felt his hair was more important than a European trip, I would find him a safe place to stay in Florida but I didn't plan to show up in Russia with a child who would immediately be pegged as a hippie. In 1970, Russians arrested hippies on sight.

When Max realized I was serious, he agreed to a haircut. He looked like a 16-year-old Beatle.

I packed our clothes, aiming for conservative, easy to care for and multi-purpose. We didn't stand out in England until we spoke. In Russia we couldn't have stood out more if we had worn suits designed for moon walks. People gave us a wide berth. I got a sense of how lepers must have felt. It was clear the average Russian feared anything American, except for small, blond American children. I was grateful we had Andrea with us. In Leningrad there were few children and the ones we did see were clearly very valuable. No child went out without an adult clutching his or her hand. Probably due to inter-breeding with Nordic stock all the children were blue-eyed blonds. Some adults had brown hair but the children were still fair.

Andrea was small and delicate with hair so blond it was almost white, and big blue eyes. Every time we got on a bus or tram some woman insisted Andrea had to sit on her lap and the woman would then pat her and say what were clearly kind and loving things in Russian and give her candy. Andrea smiled and accepted kisses and candy with polite thanks, endured numerous hugs and even hugged back. Once after climbing off a bus, she smiled and waved at the old woman who had claimed her. Then when the bus was out of sight, she turned to Pete and me and said, "Boy, if you can't speak Russian, you sure have to smile a lot."

Our hotel was directly across from a major train station. There were so few vehicles on the streets that I wasn't certain which side of the street they drove on because most drove down the middle unimpeded by any oncoming traffic. In Leningrad, we saw nothing but official vehicles. People poured in and out of the train station across from our hotel at all hours. It was impossible to guess the time by looking out at the street. Close to the summer solstice, it was never fully dark.

It was a wonderful time to be in Russia. There was no western influence whatsoever. Each time we got off the elevator on our floor, a woman sitting at an imposing desk demanded our names and had to see our room keys then noted the time in a journal before we were allowed to walk away. We had to do this in reverse before we were allowed on the elevator to go to the lobby.

I had read about the communist party policy all over Russia that made everyone put in two weeks a year doing manual work, regardless of their normal work status. The theory being that this would keep them from thinking they were better than the average working man or woman. The hotels were a testament to the ridiculous notion that the working classes weren't experts at their crafts. The people who administered this program did have the sense to be selective about some professions. The college professors didn't forge steel beams. They stuck to laying bricks, setting bathroom tiles and painting buildings. Only no one taught them how to do these jobs well. The tiles in every one of our bathrooms looked as though they had been set by someone who had never seen a wet saw. Every side started with full tiles at one corner and stopped wherever the last full tile ended. After that point, cement was used in an effort to fill the resulting void. I found it amusing. For some reason it upset the kids.

England had replicated the comfortable surroundings they had always known with a charming accent added to make the surroundings exotic enough to make them feel well-traveled. They could read the signs and buy food they recognized. Given a map, they could figure out which bus or tube line to take.

Russia was strange. The only blankets were scratchy khaki wool and looked as though they were Russian Army leftovers. Or the proverbial hair shirts beloved by masochistic medieval monks. These were encased in what looked like white cotton duvet covers with a large open diamond shape in the center. I was glad I wasn't a Russian chamber maid. It looked as though centering the thick blanket in the cover would have been an exhausting challenge.

Pete and I had a great time. We both enjoyed the strange aspects. We didn't get to see inside as many museums as we had hoped. Meals were taken seriously and took a long time to serve and eat. If we wanted to eat, we had to forego something else.

Max wanted to roam on his own. This worked in England. His friend from school had invited him to visit the Russian language institute. The boy had told him how to get there and back. The Intourist rep seemed to think this was okay. She insisted children were safe anywhere in Russia. Pete and I exchanged worried glances but neither of us said anything. Pete was the only one authorized to exchange money but any of us could spend it. He gave Max enough rubles to get through a day.

There were small liquid dispensers mounted on the outsides of buildings in downtown Leningrad and Moscow. The Intourist guide was surprised when I asked her what they were dispensing and then she was disgusted when I didn't know what kvass was. She explained it was a mildly alcoholic beverage usually made from rye bread crusts, yeast and sugar. I was tempted to ask, why only crusts? What do they do with the rest of the loaf? I really did wonder but got the impression she had a hard time dealing with American stupidity as it was.

Max was intrigued with the idea that he could buy something alcoholic by dropping a few kopecks in a coin slot. I told him this was a bad idea. There was one very sticky finger-and mouth-marked glass upended on a post. As we were looking at a kvass dispenser, a woman walked up to the machine. Her bleached blonde hair was partly covered by a well-used and rarely washed babushka so old and dirty I couldn't make out its design. She dropped her coin in the slot and pushed the glass down against what turned out to be a water spigot, not bothering to move her filthy, black finger-nailed hand from the resulting gush of cold water. She shook the glass to get every last drop of water out, lifted it, positioned it under a spout, pushed a second button and watched the glass fill with murky brown fluid. After gulping this down, she re-hung the glass and lumbered off.

I shuddered at the thought of touching the glass, let alone drinking from it and told Max I would order kvass when we ate if he wanted to taste it. He didn't seem interested.

The rest of us saw as much as we could each day. Max left after breakfast with his one day stipend and was back in time for supper. He didn't say where he had been but was clearly having a good time. This was the first country I had been in where the language was based on a completely different system and used the Cyrillic alphabet. Max was able to transpose the correct Russian sounds to letters with different pronunciations in English. I was slow at it and had to do the mental exercise letter by letter.

Leningrad was virtually unchanged since the war ended. Unlike American cities, there was no transition from worn but still elegant stone buildings built long ago to mimic buildings in Paris and open farm land. It was a chilly place made colder by canals snaking through the city and a cold wind blowing off the Baltic Sea. It was rumored to be warmer than inland Russia, which was a scary thought.

We asked to ride the train from Leningrad to Moscow but were informed we would go by air. A different Intourist guide met us in Moscow. This one told us flat out that no one bought the stupid myth that we were the parents of these children. We were too young and *nobody* had four children any more.

Max ran into this belief schism when talking with a group of English-speaking Russian students. They asked him where he lived. He described the house in Wilmette. They were so irritated at what they were certain were lies they cut him off. *No one* had a six-bedroom house. They could believe a two-bedroom flat — even *that* was probably a lying boast — but they were insulted that Max couldn't even stay within likely probabilities if he were going to lie.

At the Moscow airport, we each gave Pete our rubles. Max had far more than he should have had. Pete and I were both furious. And frightened. We knew he must have sold something, maybe some of his blue jeans. They seemed to be a ridiculously hot item in Russia. Young men had been sidling up to the boys since we arrived with offers of what seemed to me to be far too many rubles for a tired pair of jeans.

Max started out with three pairs of jeans. He did all his own packing once we started traveling. I didn't know how many were left. Our Intourist minder had made it clear that selling anything to a Russian was an immediately jail-able offense. Trying to keep his voice low, Pete asked Max what he had sold.

Max tried to look offended but he was a lousy actor. Pete flatly refused to turn in Max's rubles for American currency. My stomach knotted. I couldn't argue with Pete. He was right but we were surrounded by uniformed soldiers and I was chicken-hearted enough to wish he hadn't chosen Moscow airport to take a moral stand. The soldiers were probably nice guys but they were not just standing around with pistols in holsters in case we needed protection from bad guys. They were holding machine guns in front of their chests and looking bored as though they wished there were something fun to do like shoot ugly Americans with badly behaved children.

Max knew rubles were worthless outside Russia. No other country would exchange them in 1970. He finally realized he was going to end up with a lot of worthless paper. He set his jaw, held up the bunch of rubles so the Russian soldiers couldn't miss what he was doing, ripped the stack of bills into small pieces and dropped them in the basket meant for items we weren't allowed to take out of Russia. The hair on the back of my neck lifted. I was breathing in shallow gasps. We were the only foreigners leaving on this flight. I was certain Pete and I would be arrested. I was waiting to feel a gun barrel stuck in my back. I knew the soldiers saw the whole thing. The bulky soldier closest to us flinched. We had wandered in and out of food markets and been amazed at how much rubles bought. I imagined this was the first time the soldier saw someone tear up enough rubles to feed his family for a week. These seemed to be foot soldiers. Maybe they hadn't been instructed to respond without an officer to tell them what to do. I fervently hoped no officer strolled by and decided to make an issue of Max's destruction of government issued currency.

Panic makes time crawl at a slug's pace. I pictured scenarios where I sent Linda home with Seth and Andrea. Maybe the police would still act on their assumption the man in the family was in charge and arrest only Pete and Max. But I doubted it. Mothers were blamed for the dumb things their children did everywhere else. Why should the Russians be any different?

By the time the SAS 727 to Copenhagen was airborne, I was light-headed with relief and profoundly grateful we hadn't been able to book space on Aeroflot. After their experience on the Russian airline with its dingy broken interior and rude, doughy and shabbily dressed stewardesses, the kids were open mouthed at the slender young Scandinavian women with their rosy, fine-grained skin and shining blonde hair who greeted us with smiles. Even I fingered the bright, spotless upholstery and reveled in one more layer of safety between us and the Russian government.

Max brooded. He thought Pete was being unfair. He clearly had no idea we had narrowly escaped an extended vacation in a Russian jail.

Except for the tall glasses of sour, unflavored kefir that were a standard part of the breakfasts, the kids liked the Russian food. But they fell in love with the long, thin Danish sausages pronounced pullsa. They were similar to American hot dogs without the ensuing stomach ache or cramps. After Russia, Copenhagen seemed as sparkly fresh and clean as Disney World. We didn't hesitate to eat food from vendors' carts.

Max roamed on his own, sneering at Seth because his brother openly enjoyed the Tivoli Gardens. Max almost got us booted out of our hotel. There was only one elevator in the five-story building. It had a habit of stopping just shy of the floor. Sometimes this was enough to keep the doors from opening until someone on the first floor pushed the up button. The third day we were in Copenhagen, Max decided to fix it. We never knew what he did but it froze the elevator in place. There was only one porter, a red-faced man who looked like a stroke waiting to happen even when the elevator worked. We offered to pay for the elevator repair man. They were gracious, didn't ask us to leave but suggested we should try to control our son. Pete and I were both furious. Max tried to justify what he had done. He always did, no matter how clear it was to everyone else that he had been in the wrong. This made the rest of our stay uncomfortable. We tried to be invisible as we skulked in and out but there was always someone at the desk.

Max opted to stay at a hostel when the rest of us took four days to drive around the Danish countryside with a swing through Germany. He had developed a bad case of diarrhea. He denied trying the kvass but added if he *had* tried the kvass, the alcohol in it would have overcome the threat of contamination.

Liz, a girl he met at the school and hoped to see again, had been hospitalized for more than a week with what was first thought to be cholera but was finally determined to be just an unusually severe gastro-intestinal illness, so we may have been maligning him.

The desk clerk at the hotel in Copenhagen told me where the hospital was and said they had universal health care and would treat Max in an emergency. We dropped him off at the hostel, paid for a four-day stay and told him to eat rice, crackers and noodles and to skip fatty food and beer. Pete gave him enough money to eat. I would have liked to feel sympathy for him but he had exhausted all I had.

Chapter 47

Nova High School was in Broward County, Florida, a few miles inland from Ft. Lauderdale. The ranch house we bought was in Hollywood, the part of the county closest to Miami, where Pete and I both found work in a small advertising agency. I felt it was important to find a four bedroom house so Max and Seth didn't have to share a room but none seemed to exist in our price range. The realtor said people didn't spend enough time indoors to waste space on extra bedrooms. I could see the logic of this but I didn't like the idea of putting the boys together again.

Our house sprawled but there was still a lot of yard. A large heated pool and patio were accessed from the master bedroom. Night was my favorite time. Spicy night-blooming jasmine scented the air. A constant breeze rustled the fronds on the tall coconut palms in the side yard with a sound like something a New Age composer would play using wind instruments made by rain forest natives.

True to his promise, Pete bought a boat and trailer, enrolled us in Coast Guard safety classes for boat owners, and had a trailer hitch put on my car. He had a five speed Mustang and didn't want it near salt water. My car was an automatic drive Nash Rambler. Not my first choice but all we could afford after the Mustang and the boat. We needed two cars because I came home an hour and a half before Pete did and had to collect Andrea from the babysitter's and make dinner. I missed the public transportation we had in Wilmette.

Linda was away at college on the other side of Florida and loving it. She had chosen it because it was so far away from Wilmette. She was freaked out when we moved to Florida but relaxed when she realized we were still a long way away. She said there were a few kids at college who were almost as weird as Max, but since she wasn't related to them she didn't have to bother with them or be embarrassed by their antics.

Andrea and I went on a few boat trips but then I opted to mow the grass and stay home unless we were water-skiing or actually going somewhere. The boat was parked in our driveway and launched from a ramp on an inlet a few miles from the house. Every time it was launched there were arguments. The boring job of vacuuming the pool beat dealing with three males fighting to be the one in charge.

Without Max, Pete and Seth were always peaceful together but if they even tried to drive up to Fort Lauderdale to buy the Sunday Times without Max, he flew out of the house so fearful he would miss something, he literally looked as though his flailing arms and legs were operating without the benefit of the rest of his body. This made me feel sad. But there was nothing I could do to change the underlying chemistry. Pete and Seth meshed without effort. Pete and Max were like oil and water, where someone forgot the emulsifier to make them bind together. Their relationship was simply bad chemistry.

On an earlier vacation Pete had suggested we all get certified as scuba divers. We bought scuba gear, signed up for a course and all of us but Andrea, became certified divers. Andrea swam with the agility and confidence of an eager minnow but was too small to wear a regulation tank.

When we moved to Florida she complained about being left out. Max seemed to identify with this. He put on his tank and mask, found a mask small enough for her to wear and showed her how to buddy dive in our pool. I was surprised to see how patient he was with her. Fortunately, she was a quick learner. They continued until the tank was empty.

By January, we had done all the fun things we could think of so many times they had become routine.

Seth was the only one who had found friends. The agency Pete had worked for in Philadelphia and for the first five years we were in Wilmette asked him to go to Seattle to supervise the shooting of a commercial for an account he had worked on and knew well. He jumped at the chance. I envied him. He would be surrounded by witty, creative people whose minds sparked each other's thoughts.

Pete decided Florida was a great place to own a motorcycle and bought a Honda 70 because it met the below five horsepower limit for under-16-year-old drivers. He planned to give it to Seth when he turned 15 in April and got his learner's permit. In the meantime, it was going to be another family fun toy. He was irritated when I said I had no desire to ride a motorcycle. He nagged at me for being a spoilsport so one Sunday I rode on the back of the motorcycle to an empty school parking lot. Riding on any vehicle with my knees sticking out where one of the old people who drove around Florida in the dead center of the road going either too fast or too slow could take off one of my kneecaps made me a lousy back seat passenger. I kept flinching.

The bike wasn't powerful but it was large and heavy. I could carry the other side of two sheets of dry wall and hoist 50-pound sacks of cement but at five-foot-three and 110 pounds, I had my limits. The first was obvious. My legs were too short for this bike. When I tried to keep the bike upright when it wasn't moving, it canted at such an acute angle I was holding up most of its considerable weight. Pete insisted I could ride it if I tried. So I tried. I got it started. I even rode it around the lot a few times more than I wanted to because I knew if I stopped I had to get my left leg on the ground and hold the bike up. I finally stopped, was able to get the kick stand open and climbed off. That was it. I explained I would rather be a spoilsport than crippled.

Florida was every motorcycle-obsessed kid's dream state. With a learner's permit, they could legally ride a motorcycle on city streets. Seth considered the motorcycle his but Max got to it before Seth reached his fifteenth birthday. Pete said Max could ride it to school and signed the permission form. I cringed every time he rode off on it. He couldn't get to the first corner without gunning it a few times and executing a wheelie.

I had just arrived at work at the advertising agency one morning when the nurse from Nova High School called. Max had been in a motorcycle accident and was on the way to Fort Lauderdale hospital. She said he had been injured but she didn't know how seriously. She gave me the name of the hospital and told me how to get there. Pete was in Seattle so I was on my own.

Thank God I spent so much of my life behind the wheel of a car and was able to call on muscle memory to automatically respond to the traffic. My heart pounded and it was hard to breathe. I was in total panic mode for the next hour. I know I drove from Miami to Fort Lauderdale then located the hospital and retained the school nurse's directions because I ended up in the correct emergency room, but I don't remember any of the trip.

Max's first words were garbled because his front teeth were obviously missing and blood was dribbling out of his mouth. He turned to Steve, the friend who had driven him to the hospital and said, "See, I told you she wouldn't cry."

He sounded triumphant. He told me later he knew how upset I was but he counted on my staying calm no matter what happened when *he* needed help. Max said he had always assumed that was what all mothers did until Steve regaled him with his own mother's hysterical melt-down reactions to some of his escapades.

Max held out his hand knowing I would hold it. There was no one else there to comfort me *or* Max so I concentrated on helping him get through what was clearly going to be a tough ordeal.

A doctor came into the room with x-rays, stuck them in a viewing frame and turned on the light. When I identified myself he said, "Max has a broken collarbone but most of the force of the impact was absorbed by his face. The bone holding his front teeth in place was shattered and five teeth were knocked out." He handed me a plastic bag with four bloodied teeth in it. He indicated Steve. "Max's friend found these and brought them up to the ER. A fifth tooth is gone but he said these were all he could find. We have a dental surgeon waiting. He'll tell you if these teeth can be implanted. Max has had a shot that should keep him moderately comfortable until you can get this filled." He handed me a prescription and a paper with directions to the surgeon's office then took the x-rays off the screen, put them back in the envelope and gave them to me.

The dental surgeon looked distressed when he looked at the x-rays. Max's mouth was beginning to swell and was obviously quite painful. The surgeon explained it would be impossible to numb his mouth adequately. "I can't afford to wait until he can be properly anesthetized. I have to get the loose bone fragments out while they're still movable. I'm sorry, Max."

It took two hours of agony to get the last bone shard out. The missing tooth had been pushed up into the bone. I was glad Steve had gone back to school so Max didn't have to maintain his bravado in front of his friend. Max had the bad luck to have unusually sensitive teeth. Pain and the remaining effects of severe shock triggered recurring nausea. He held my hands and I did what I could to comfort him but the surgeon had to give him brief time-outs to vomit blood and regroup his resources. When I showed the surgeon the pathetic little bag of bloodied but otherwise perfect front teeth and asked if he could implant them, he gestured me around so I could look into the wreck of Max's mouth and shook his head. "Too much bone gone. There's nothing left to attach them to."

That was when I almost lost it. A gaping red hole with jagged, splayed out shards of broken bone was all that was left of Max's beautiful front teeth. I couldn't even see any remaining gum. There was just shattered bone. Max had his eyes closed so he didn't see my stricken expression. I couldn't trust myself to speak. I just nodded and went back behind him.

The surgeon said, "The bottom teeth are loose but the braces should keep them in place and they'll tighten. I assume he had braces on the top teeth at one time. When did they come off?"

"Ten days ago."

The surgeon shook his head. "Probably a good thing they were off. The bone above his upper teeth took most of the force. If anything, the braces would have transmitted that to his back teeth and loosened them too."

Seth was devastated. The freedom the motorcycle would have meant for him was lost for good. He knew Pete wouldn't buy another one.

Chapter 48

Max discovered he wouldn't get credit for two of the courses he had taken at New Trier because the grades he got were too low to transfer. He had to finish both the spring semester and the one next fall to get his high school degree. Already depressed by the change in his face because of the missing front teeth and the loss of the junked motorcycle, this was more than he could handle. This was his fourth year in high school. He was seventeen and weary of dealing with a world where he had to get a permission slip to go to the bathroom. He showed up at school each day but he no longer cared whether he passed or failed.

Without front teeth he sounded like a lisping caricature of an old man so he didn't speak. When he was called on by teachers, he just shrugged and looked away without answering. No one seemed to grasp how traumatic it was for a seventeen-year-old boy to suddenly lose all of his front teeth. At a time in his life when image was vital to him and his peers, he had gone from very good looking to what he was sure was glaringly ugly. He couldn't eat normal food because it was too painful to chew anything with more substance than scrambled eggs. He perfected the bored teenager expression so his teachers assumed he was just being willful.

His advisor suggested a meeting. It took us a while to set up a meeting time because Pete was away more than at home. The Seattle job for the Philadelphia agency was followed by others. The first day Pete was in town we met with the advisor.

Nova High School was a well-thought-of alternative school. I assumed this meant they would tolerate students with non-rote learning styles as long as the student learned the needed material. I had met Max's advisor before and had the impression he liked Max. He began by telling us Max was surly and uncoop- erative in his classes. He discounted the impact of the visible injury to his face and the resulting loss to his self-esteem. For reasons that never made sense to me, the advisor had decided all Max's problems stemmed from a total lack of discipline at home.

"You should tell him 'No' and mean it. He needs to be disciplined when he behaves in an inappropriate manner."

He knew Pete was away a lot so he addressed most of his remarks to me. I was unconsciously shaking my head. My mouth was slack with surprise. I hadn't expected this total lack of understanding. He stopped speaking, frowned and said, "You don't agree with me?"

The challenge in his voice infuriated me. I felt like screaming but made an effort to answer quietly. My voice shook with pent-up frustration.

"I agree in principle. But saying 'No' only works if the person you're saying 'No' to agrees with your assumption you have the right to make all the rules. Max doesn't just disagree with most rules; he doesn't even acknowledge they exist."

He looked at me with a dismissive expression. I could see I had presented him with a concept beyond his experience. "What you have to do is make it clear to Max you will withhold something he really cares about if he doesn't follow your rules."

Pete answered in a hard, bitter voice. "Short of taking his life, I can't think of anything we could take from him he would care about enough not to do exactly what he wanted. And there are days even that threat wouldn't stop him."

I nodded in agreement.

Max's school had a three-day weekend for President's Day. He asked if he could go camping in the Everglades. Two boys in his German class were going and wanted him to go with them because he knew how to camp. One of the boys had an old Fiat. They would use that if they could fit all their camping gear in it. It didn't need much gas.

Pete and I talked it over. He was in Seattle this time. Max was an experienced camper. We agreed it would be a nice change for him to be the expert in something for a change. The boy's Fiat had some problem that couldn't be fixed in time to take advantage of the President's Day holiday.

Max asked if he could borrow the Ford van we had bought when my car developed too many problems to feel safe commuting in and out of Miami. Pete thought this was okay. He told Max he had to do all the driving because our insurance wouldn't cover any driver under 25 except for family members. I reiterated this and Max assured me it wouldn't be a problem. The campsite was only a couple of hours' drive away.

He showed me a map of the Everglades and indicated the camping ground where the boys would be. He collected camping and fishing gear and went to pick up the other boys. I had made dozens of cookies and sent these with him.

The peace was wonderful. He showed up exactly when he had said he would and unloaded the camping gear.

And the motorcycle he had to abandon in Illinois last spring.

***

I couldn't process what I was seeing. Then I looked at Max and recognized the expression of guilty defiance. "You went to Illinois?"

He put his hands on his hips and assumed his head back, hooded eyes, hard-mouthed teen, screw-you posture. "Yeah. What did you expect me to do? I have no way to get around. You wouldn't help me get my motorcycle when you could have. You don't think I was going to leave it in Illinois forever, do you?"

I felt so sick it was hard to think. I heard myself nibbling the edges of what felt like a major betrayal. Minutia came out of my mouth. "The other boys drove?"

"Of course. You didn't think I could drive that long without any relief, did you?"

"Why did the boys go to Illinois with you?"

220

"They had business in Chicago."

"Do they actually go to school with you?"

He was showing the beginnings of anxiety at this question. "They know a girl in my German class. They needed a ride to and from Chicago."

"Why? Were they from Chicago?"

"No. They just had to make a delivery."

Max was still bad at keeping a blank face. He was clearly uneasy. Something was off about this whole scenario. I had a mental image of two 17-year-olds but I never saw his alleged classmates. They could have been grown men. Why wouldn't they have cars of their own? Maybe they were transporting dope and didn't want to be in a vehicle one of them owned that could be seized if they were pulled over.

"Were they moving dope?"

Max made a small movement of indifference but didn't answer. I felt that awful sensation usually described as a sinking heart. Mine felt as though it was trying to get to my feet. I hunched forward and cradled my middle as though I really had to hold it in place.

"Max, I know you think the marijuana laws are unfair but you drove through a lot of states to get to Chicago. Some of them still have draconian laws regarding possession of dope. You could end up in jail for getting caught with one joint. God knows what they would do if you were knowingly carrying a sizable quantity. You *do* know if someone stopped you and found dope, you'd not only end up in jail but they'd confiscate the car?"

"No one stopped us. We were careful to stay within the speed limit."

At that point, I would have given Max to anyone who happened by but there wasn't much of a market for out-of-control teenage boys.

I was so overwhelmed by the enormity of what Max had done, I had to mentally step sideways to give my mind time to cope with it. I had a family to care for. So I washed clothes, shopped, cooked, made sure Seth did his homework, read Andrea stories, went to work and was as careful as usual to do a good job.

But I felt as though a part of me was dying.

No one noticed.

Chapter 49

Shortly after Max got what looked like half of an upper set of false teeth, Liz from the language school in Leningrad visited us. She was charming, funny in an offhand way and attractive. I could see why Max liked her. I asked her if she could stay for dinner. She said, "Sure. My grandmother isn't expecting me. Max said you always feed anyone who happens to be in the house around dinner time."

I laughed. Every time Max came up with an accurate observation about someone else's thinking, I was surprised. I started to cook and realized I needed butter and milk. When I left, Andrea was sitting in the family room watching TV with Max and Liz. Max was becoming more and more brazen in his defiance of other people's rights. I would normally insist Andrea come with me if I went to the grocery store but I assumed Liz would intercede if Max was mean to Andrea. Seth was in the living room playing pool with a friend. Pete would be home for dinner soon. He was in Miami this week. I figured nothing could go wrong with so many people in the house and I would only be gone for 20 minutes at most.

The grocery store was crowded; I was gone for almost an hour. I knew something was wrong the minute I stepped out of the car. Seth was yelling and I heard pounding. The noise sounded in sync with Seth's shrieks — I assumed he was the one assaulting what sounded like a closed door. I found him outside the bedroom he shared with Max. He was whacking the door yelling, "Let me in. Open the damn door. You have no right to lock me out."

Seth's face was red, his voice hoarse. Furious, he looked on the verge of tears.

"What's wrong? Why are you yelling?"

"They're in *my* room screwing." He banged the door again. It bowed slightly each time he hit it. He's strong. I was surprised it was still on its hinges. He whipped around and shrieked. "Do something. Don't I have *any* rights in this house?"

Seth had his arm cocked ready to bang on the door when Max unlocked the door and opened it. Seth reared back as though confronting a monster.

Max looked smug. He made a point of zipping his fly *after* he stepped out of the room.

I turned on him. "WHAT THE HELL WERE YOU DOING? HOW CAN YOU BE SO THOUGHTLESS? THAT'S SETH'S ROOM TOO. WHAT MAKES YOU THINK IT'S ALL RIGHT TO HAVE SEX IN THE ROOM YOU SHARE WITH YOUR BROTHER?"

I knew they could probably hear me at the other end of town but I felt so outraged I couldn't stop screaming.

"Where else can I do it? You took the van. You don't expect me to go around with blue balls just because I don't have a hotel room, do you?"

Liz came out of the boys' bedroom. She was fully dressed but her cardigan had been buttoned so rapidly one side dangled below the other side like a kindergarten kid's. She looked detached and pleased with herself, clearly post-coital, not a bit upset or guilty.

Pete walked in. "What's all the yelling about? I could hear you at the other end of the block.

Seth swung around, "They were screwing in *my* room."

Pete's face turned red and seemed to swell. He stared at Liz. He started shrieking at her. "YOU FUCKING CUNT. GET THE FUCK OUT OF MY HOUSE."

Liz looked surprised. She rolled her eyes but had the sense to leave without comment. Pete glared at Max but didn't say anything to him then stormed out to the family room, poured a generous belt of Dewars over ice, walked back to our bedroom and slammed the door.

Andrea's door was closed. I tapped on it and opened it when I heard a muffled reply. I couldn't figure out what she said but I wanted to reassure her all the hassle was over. She was curled up on her bed with her hands clamped over her ears and the worn-out bunny she always slept with clutched under her elbow. The seven-year-old girl had lived her whole life in Max's dark shadow. I sat down next to her and scratched her back.

"I'm sorry about that whole ugly scene, Andrea. I wish Max had more sense."

"Why did Dad yell at Liz? Why didn't he yell at Max too?" She sniffed and looked up at me. Her eyes were red and the lids were swollen. She had been crying for some time.

I felt sad. She shouldn't have had to deal with this crazy, out-of-control behavior. I knew 17-year-olds were infamous for their capacity to be self-absorbed but this was too far beyond the end point of normal behavior. I wasn't sure what to say. I didn't fault Max for wanting sex with a willing girl. He had said Liz was already 18 and added she was emancipated. I had assumed at the time he meant she was no longer a virgin but with Max I was never sure what he was really telling me. Most kids had the smarts to find a place more private than the bedroom they shared with their brother. Seth was 14 and well aware of his own sexuality. I wondered how much of Max's choice of a place to have sex had to do with lording his sexual maturity over his brother.

Pete always told me I read too much into things that were really just what they seemed to be. He was a strong believer in Occam's razor. I thought Occam's philosophy was classic male avoidance thinking. Any woman knew that what you saw was often just the tip of a tentacle belonging to a large treacherous octopus waiting to suck you into its world.

I normally defended Pete but I agreed with Andrea. Pete shouldn't have attacked Liz so violently and obscenely and ignored Max's culpability. The implications of what he said offended me too. I snuggled against her, scratched her back then stroked her head.

She reached over and patted my arm. We sat nestled together offering each other comfort. I bent down and kissed her cheek. "Would you like to come into the kitchen with me and help me make supper? You can peel the carrots and I'll cut you some carrot pennies to eat."

"Are you going to cook the carrots the way Dad likes with the brown sugar and onions?"

"No. I'm doing them the way the kids like for a change." She glanced at me. I hoped I didn't sound as irritated as I felt.

"Where's Max?"

"I think he's with Seth and Pete watching TV. Don't worry. I'll be here. You can stay with me."

No one said much during dinner. I was simmering. Why *did* Pete attack Liz with such venom and let Max go unscathed? It was sending the wrong message to give all three kids. I waited until Andrea was tucked into bed, Seth was in his room doing homework and Max had gone out. My car was still in the driveway so someone had picked him up. I assumed it was Liz but didn't ask. Pete was watching TV.

I stood not more than six feet away from him with my arms crossed on my chest. I knew this was a defensive posture. Irritated with myself, I dropped my arms to my sides and tried to look more confident. Unease forced my arms back where they had been. I hated confronting Pete. He knew I was there but he wouldn't acknowledge me.

I finally forced myself to say, "Are you going to give Max a lecture about respecting other people's rights or let him think this was all Liz's fault?"

I was so angry by now my voice was wobbly.

He turned up the volume on the TV. When he realized his rudeness wasn't going to drive me from the room, he looked at me with open disgust. "It *was* her fault. If that fucking whore

226

hadn't come on to him, he wouldn't have been screwing her."

I clenched my teeth. "That's the most sexist thing I've ever heard..."

Before I could finish my sentence, he bolted out of the chair, slammed the off switch on the TV, snatched the keys to his car from the key rack and lunged out the door. It slammed behind him. I heard the car shoot out of the driveway. He was already going too fast.

He left for Philadelphia early the next morning. He drove himself to the airport. I doubt if he wanted to be trapped in a car with me.

Chapter 50

"Just a minute. Just a minute." I assumed the person knocking on my door couldn't hear me but I didn't want to shout and wake the kids. The light on the clock read 2:32. Damn. I had only been asleep for a few hours. Pete was still asleep. I didn't wake him. After the ugly incident with Liz, we were barely speaking. I avoided him as much as possible. It wasn't hard. He was someplace else most of the time.

If one of Max's friends was banging on my door; he was dead meat. I was tired of being polite to people who didn't return the courtesy. Max seemed to be drawn to boys who never slept during normal hours and didn't care if other people wanted to.

I grabbed a robe, stuffed my arms into it, trotted to the side door and flicked on the outside light. My heart took a nasty leap. For a few seconds it felt as though it was lodged against my windpipe in a thwarted effort to get out of my chest cavity. This was trouble again.

A tired-looking car was parked at the end of my driveway. The red light on the roof was the only indication it was a police car. The light wasn't turned on. Maybe it was just a cop warning us about a prowler. It flashed through my mind that it was a sad commentary on my life when a loose prowler was good news. When I opened the door, I saw that the man standing there wasn't in uniform. He was wearing a rumpled and not too clean jacket with what looked like a piece of candy wrapper stuck to the fabric above the right pocket. A bulge under his left arm was obviously a holstered pistol. A large one. Sparse ginger hair was such a close color match for his florid face it was hard to see where it began and ended. He pulled open the screen door and stepped in, crowding me so I had to step back. He asked me who I was. His voice was flat, official, wary. He was tense. He eyed me as though expecting me to whip out a gun.

I was duly intimidated but irritation over-rode any anxiety. I got very cranky when someone large bullied me. I fought down my impulse to snarl at him. I knew this wasn't about me. I fell back on super-polite and told him my name in one of those simpering, super-polite voices better suited to a garden party than a confrontation with a policeman. I couldn't quite manage the pasted-on smile that should have gone with the voice. It was just as well. He wasn't in the mood to notice nuances.

He flashed a badge, said his name and identified himself as a detective. "Are you the owner of a white 1971 Ford van?" He rattled off the license number. He spoke with the nasal, southern twang I associated with Florida natives from the vast farms in the interior of the state. It took me a second to figure out what he had just said.

I shrugged. "I own a van but don't know the license number."

This clearly irritated him. "Do you know where your car is?"

I automatically went to the side window so I could see beyond the boat. No car. "I have no idea."

"You weren't driving it tonight?"

"No. The last time I drove it was when I went to the baby sitter's to pick up my daughter at four o'clock this afternoon."

A second police car drove up. This time the officer was in uniform and his red and white flashers were broadcasting their message of alarm across all the white stucco houses on our corner. He tapped on the door. I let him in. He nodded to me but didn't identify himself. His eyes were cold.

I turned back to the detective. "Why were you asking me about my car?"

The two men exchanged glances. "Is there anyone who could have been driving your car without your knowledge?"

"What is this about? Is someone hurt?" I was suddenly flooded with guilt. What if I was thinking dark thoughts about Max and his inconsiderate friends and he had been in an accident or hurt? "Please. Tell me what happened."

The detective narrowed his eyes as though trying to see me clearly. I must have looked like the suddenly frightened mother I was, because his voice sounded kinder.

"We responded to an alarm at a construction site near the high school and found an empty car registered in your name up against a chain link fence. Someone had been trying to break into a shack where dynamite was stored."

Feeling like a pricked balloon, I reached for the arm of a chair and eased myself into it before I ended up on the floor. "No sign of the driver?"

"No. That's why we're here. We've impounded the car. We need to know who was driving."

I took a deep breath and stood slowly. "Let me check." I started back to the boys' bedroom.

"I'm afraid we'll have to come with you, ma'am."

I led the way back to Max's room. As he did every night, Max had left an opened wax paper package of Graham crackers out on the kitchen counter. When I flicked on the light one of the enormous roaches the natives euphemistically called palmetto bugs shot out of the wrapping around the crackers, across the table and dropped to the floor with a click. Forgetting I hadn't taken time to put on shoes, I stomped it with my bare heel before it could get under the counter then shuddered. I left the smashed cockroach on the floor, picked up the crackers and dumped them into the waste basket and continued into the living room.

The pool table we had hauled from Illinois was in the center of the room. Both men looked at it with obvious appreciation. The uniformed officer lightly ran his fingers across the green felt and muttered, "Wow."

The detective looked at me with raised eyebrows. Before either man could ask, I said, "We inherited the table and this is the only room large enough to accommodate it."

There was a subtle shift in their attitude toward me. A woman who allowed the living room to be used as a pool hall couldn't be all bad.

Max was sitting on his bed, fully dressed and holding the car keys. He tried to look belligerent but was doing a bad job of it. The detective looked at a paper he pulled out of his coat pocket, read off a license number then spelled out all the details of the site where the car was found and asked Max if he was driving a white Ford van with the plate number he read off and had abandoned it at this site.

Max answered, "Yes, sir," in an unsteady voice.

By then Seth was awake. He looked interested but not surprised.

The detective asked to see Max's driver's license.

Max had to stand to get his wallet out of his pocket. His movements were awkward. I knew what he was doing but the policemen tensed. The detective stepped far enough away to be beyond the range of Max's arms. The uniformed officer put his right hand on his still-holstered revolver in a reflexive gesture.

They relaxed when Max finally fumbled his wallet out of his pocket, flapped it open and handed it to the detective.

The detective pulled the license out of the plastic sleeve, read it and said,

"You're seventeen?"

"Yes sir." Max's voice was steadier now. The bravado he had tried to project earlier was in place now. He had noticed Seth was awake and watching with interest. He couldn't let his brother see him cower in front of officials he insisted on calling pigs. I fervently hoped he had the sense not to call a Florida cop by that label. This was definitely not Wilmette and we weren't even in the high end of this town where we might have been approached with more caution. Both detectives jumped when a tall, barefoot man with too-long hair and an irritated expression on his bearded face suddenly appeared in the doorway behind them.

The detective gave me a wary look. "Who's this? You didn't tell me there was someone else here."

Before I could say anything, Seth said, "He's our father."

The detective frowned at me. "You have a husband?"

I nodded. He looked at me with a quizzical expression on his face. "Why didn't you get your husband before you opened the door?"

I thought of a bunch of replies. But decided I would be better off not saying anything since, "Why would I do that? I usually deal with the police," was the real reason and I didn't think that would help Max. So I just kept my face politely blank.

He ignored me after that until I had to sign papers admitting he had told me where my car was being held, how to reclaim it and how much I would be charged for each day it was in the pound.

Pete had to sign everything else. This was the good side of being relegated to subservient wife status.

Max was handcuffed, ushered into the backseat of the patrolman's car and taken to the County jail. He would be arraigned and formally charged early the following morning.

Chapter 51

Pete and I sat on the hard bench in the Broward County court room without talking. After Max had been driven off in the police car, we had spent the rest of the night pacing restlessly. Pete asked if I wanted a cup of coffee, Pete code for, "Make me a cup of coffee," but I just shook my head. He knew how to make coffee as well as I did. I didn't have the energy for macho games.

My brain was filled with terrifying images of Max being gang-raped. Or stabbed or beaten because he resisted. Would he be dumped into the general population?

Or would the police put him with kids his age? He was still 17. Not that this would necessarily keep him safe. Florida was a year-round scum magnet. Some of the kids I saw lurking downtown at night were too young to shave but looked as threatening as the most vicious felons in Hollywood movies.

When it was finally time to get ready for court, I grabbed the plainest dress I owned, shoved my sandals aside and opted for pantyhose and low-heeled pumps. This wasn't the time for a fashion statement.

I felt hollow inside but I couldn't eat. We talked about lawyers on the drive to the court. We didn't know what sort of lawyer we should get or what the actual charge would be. Was this a local, state, or federal crime? Did it make any difference that he was still underage? Pete said we might as well wait until after the arraignment so we knew what we needed before we called our lawyer friend in Philadelphia for a referral to someone we could trust. The lawyer had gone to law school at Duke University and knew attorneys all over the south.

A scattering of people slumped on the uncomfortable courtroom seats with expressions of brooding resentment or hopeless resignation. The struggling air conditioning spewed out cold air tinged with an odor somewhere between moldy towels and used gym socks.

Pete and I both stiffened and jerked our heads to face the open side door when the sound of chains clanking in a slow, rhythmic cadence accompanied by an odd shuffling noise came from the hall. A man with the muscle-thickened torso of a wrestler and short bandy legs burst through the open door and strutted into the courtroom. Patches of sweat already darkened the armpits of his starched brown uniform. A holstered gun rode his hip. His red face had fat, shiny cheeks and an improbably small nose. Aviator sunglasses hid his eyes. The clanking shuffle grew louder. The first prisoner appeared at the door. I gasped and my vision wavered as though someone had just given me a bare-knuckled punch in the gut. The prisoner's face was so bruised and swollen he was unrecognizable. But it wasn't Max. His hair was too short and the wrong color. His raw-knuckled hands were cuffed in front of him. A leg-iron on his left ankle was chained to one on his right leg then linked to the man behind him and to the next man and the next. They all wore neon-orange jumpsuits that probably came in different sizes but made everyone look equally shapeless. The prisoners ended up in a wobbly line facing the raised dais at the front of the room. Clumped together by the leg irons, their faces were hard to see unless they turned and looked at the spectators. Black, white, Hispanic, fat, thin, burly. I couldn't see Max. Had something happened to him? He wouldn't have had the sense to be quiet if someone challenged him. What if he had been beaten and was in the hospital?

I leaned forward and gripped the edge of the hard bench. Panic made it hard to see. I took a series of deep breaths and looked at each of the men's backs one by one. He wasn't there. One of the men straightened and pulled his shoulders back. I caught the movement out of the corner of my eyes. But he was too tall. I was about to look away when he turned his head as the man next to him said something. Tears filled my eyes. When had Max gotten so tall? His mouth was clamped in a hard line. I didn't see any cuts or bruises. If he were frightened or intimidated, it didn't show. I slumped back in relief.

The tethered men were mostly a seedy lot. A few obvious drunks, a few with dirty, unshaven faces and grease-stiffened dreadlocks. One lost-looking soul hummed an atonal chant and would have collapsed in a heap if he hadn't been chained between two other men. The vomit-tinged stench of unwashed bodies oozed across the courtroom and enfolded the watchers in the sordid spectacle. Three of the men looked surly and bored, as though they knew the drill and couldn't get too worked up about it.

Max didn't look to see if we were there. He never said if that was because he was afraid we were there or afraid we weren't. I didn't ask.

The man in front of Max was fat, white and could have been anywhere between 18 and 40. He had tattoos on all visible surfaces and the face of a nasty boy who enjoyed pulling wings off butterflies. The man behind Max had skin so black it had navy shadows. He was tall, wide without being fat, had a high cheek-boned face and looked like he should have been behind a desk. The white man looked aggrieved and sulky, the black man resigned and disgusted.

A lawyer wearing a good suit stood behind him. The proceedings went smoothly. There were two men and one woman who looked as though they could have been court appointed-lawyers and a man who turned out to be a bail bondsman. We couldn't hear much of what was being said. A few men were led to a room off the courtroom. They were handed labeled bags that must have held their own clothing and other belongings. They came back to the courtroom minus the orange jumpsuits. The black man and his lawyer walked out the front door. A white man in a vomit-flecked blue leisure suit shuffled out behind a hard-faced woman with brassy blond hair. She was haranguing him in a flat Bronx accent. The other men were processed one by one. Most left by a back door, still shackled, cuffed and wearing orange.

The judge gathered his papers, stared at Max then conferred with the bandy legged man. Pete and I were the only spectators left in the courtroom. The judge looked at us, shrugged then stood up and walked through a door behind the bench. The court stenographer picked up her machine and left. Max was standing alone. Pete and I walked forward. Pete asked the man who had been presenting the cases why Max wasn't called. The man riffled through his papers and said, "That's weird, there's no paperwork for him. That doesn't happen often. Are you the parents?" When we nodded, he said, "What's he charged with?" Pete told him.

"Okay. That explains why there aren't any papers for him yet. Anything to do with dynamite is a federal offense. Were the arresting officers local?"

Pete and I both nodded.

"His papers are probably still sitting in some guy's in-box. We can't hold him without the paperwork from them. The clerk will give you a temporary release. You can take him home for now. Just make sure he doesn't leave the area."

Max listened to the man but looked too exhausted to react. The uniformed man unlocked the handcuffs and leg shackles and led Max through the door where the men who were released had been taken earlier.

We found the clerk who was supposed to prepare the papers for Max's temporary release. He was probably around 50. White with fine features almost lost in whisky-reddened cheeks, he reminded me of my grandmother's third husband who spoke with the same distinctive twang and referred to himself as a Florida cracker. Many of the men working in the courthouse looked as though they came from the same background. No matter how many Northerners flocked to Florida, the apparatus that ran it was still southern at the core. The clerk shook his head and looked pensive.

"Poor kid. He's got rotten timing. Playing with dynamite's federal now. Used to be covered by Florida statute. Back then, if your boy got caught playing with dynamite, he'd most likely get a lecture and maybe have to rake the grass in the park downtown for a month or so after school. Not now. I don't think Feds were ever kids. They're not good on paperwork but they don't quit."

Pete said, "What if we take him to another state?"

The man shook his head. "Won't matter. No matter where he goes, the Feds'll come after him." He frowned, clutched his chin and mashed his mouth together. "Unless..."

I was holding my breath. Pete was suddenly rigid, all his energy concentrated on the man's words. We both stared at him.

"The boy's seventeen. How tall is he?"

Pete said, "Not much below my height. Maybe five eleven."

"Think he'd consider going into the service? That's the only place the Feds will leave him be."

Pete nodded. His expression lightened. "He's been talking about that. Wants to be a paratrooper."

"Well, see if you can get him into the army before they find the paperwork. It's Friday. I'd try to get him in the Army before Tuesday. You don't want him to end up in any prison in Florida: state *or* federal. He'll be thrown in with bad people with nothing to lose. They ruin young boys."

Pete and Max dropped me off and went to the recruiter's office. The war in Vietnam was winding down but they still wanted warm bodies. They tested him, saw his IQ and tried to talk him into taking the GED and getting a college education at their expense.

We were gnawing our nails and flinching every time a car stopped in front of our house. The enlistment process was going too slowly. Pete said he was afraid to tell the recruiter why it was important to get Max signed up and on a bus. They might not want someone who had been arrested. Friday slid by. Recruiters worked weekends but couldn't do anything until they got his high school transcript. Monday was counted off second by second. We were all wrecks. Supper time came and Max was still a civilian.

Someone pounded on the front door at eight on Tuesday morning. I was afraid to go to the door — I knew beyond a doubt that I would see a Federal officer, holstered gun on his hip and handcuffs attached to his belt. When he knocked again, Andrea shrieked, "Mom, there's someone at the door. Should I get it?"

Feeling defeated, I walked to the door. I had to fight back tears of relief when I saw the mailman with a special delivery package for Pete. I couldn't thank him. I was afraid to open my mouth for fear I would start blubbering.

Pete finally told the recruiter why speed was so important. The recruiter shook his head. He said, "It isn't as though your boy was arrested for trying to break into a jewelry store. Dynamite! Good Lord! Half the enlisted men and a good few of the officers my age or older wouldn't be in the Army if that was illegal. Just means he's normal." They had Max signed up and in line for the bus to Fort Jackson at four o'clock Tuesday afternoon.

Max loved basic training. He hadn't jumped out of any airplanes or handled guns by the time he was free to call us. He was exhausted but so thrilled to be doing exactly what he had dreamed of doing, he could hardly talk in sentences.

Ten days after he left for Fort Jackson, a hard-faced, uniformed federal official showed up at our front door to arrest Max. He was so furious when I told him Max was in the army I wondered if he had some sort of quota he had to reach. Fortunately, the court official had suggested we get a copy of Max's enlistment papers to show the person who came to re-arrest him. I gathered this wasn't an unusual request because the recruiter was happy to make the copy without question.

The Federal official wanted corroboration that Max had actually gone to Fort Jackson. He insisted on coming inside the house while I got Max's first letter with the Army base postmark.

He clearly felt I was a possible felon and planned to dart out the back door and disappear if he didn't watch me. The officer looked at the pool table and the rack of pool cues on the wall . "Why do you have a regulation pool table in your living room?" His eyes were narrowed as though he had just caught me breaking some obscure law.

I felt as though I were two people. One was afraid what I said could harm Max so I had to be careful; the other was furious some officious man could walk into my house and feel he had the right to question me. Thinking Max had a lot to answer for, irritation won out. "Why we have it isn't your concern and no."

"No, what?"

"Only our friends use the table and they don't bet."

"I didn't ask that."

"You didn't ask but it would have been the next thing out of your mouth."

He wanted to take the only letter Max had mailed from camp but I said, "No." My voice was abrupt. "It's been through the U.S. mail so it's *my* property. You can confirm he's a soldier stationed at Fort Jackson with one phone call."

I held out my hand. His face got red but he slapped the letter into my palm. He slammed the front door muttering the threat that Max better be where I said he was or he'd be back and *then* I'd know what *real* trouble was.

Lying to a federal officer was a felony.

Chapter 52

Pete was offered a contract with the agency in Philadelphia. Seth was the only one in the family who wanted to stay in Florida. He had finished his first year of high school and made friends. Andrea was thrilled to leave. The principal of her grade school was allowed to spank pupils and did so. She spent most of second grade trying to be so perfect she was invisible. It was a strain she said she didn't need. We bought a house in Pennsylvania and decided to take a two-month camping trip to Alaska. We all knew the vacation was our way to celebrate the fact that Max was somewhere else and as happy to be free of us as we were to be free of him. Having finished her first year of college, Linda was embarrassed to tell her friends she was spending the summer camping with her family but thrilled at the idea of exploring what it would be like to be part of a normal family.

Our first stop was Fort Jackson. We found a campsite near the Army facility and visited Max. Tanned and already putting on muscle, he was the happiest I had ever seen him. He had inherited my early rising genes, had no problem with being rousted out of bed before dawn and was looking forward to being paid to play with guns. Already scheduled for jump school, he was slated to end up in Germany. Max had finally found a home where his peers thought loving guns and explosives was normal.

Seth says he still remembers how guilty he felt to be so relieved that he would finally be free of Max's oppressive presence. We all felt some guilt but it didn't stop us from enjoying the fact that we would be without the force of his vibrating personality crowding us into a corner. Linda and I had a great time. We shared a similar sense of the ridiculous and hadn't had much recent time together to express it.

Seth had his learner's permit. All the way across the flat

southern plains and up the west coast, Seth repeatedly asked Pete if he could drive for a while. Pete said, "No," until we came to what looked like a rarely used gravel road along the western edge of the Frazer River Canyon in Canada when he told Seth he could drive. Seth was surprised but he changed places with Pete. At the time of the shift, the fast-moving river was in a wide gully no more than three or four feet below the road and there was no oncoming traffic. We were heading north with the river on our right.

The road lost its benign appearance within the next few miles. Already narrow, it seemed to be shrinking and the canyon getting deeper much too fast. Seth's knuckles were white. Pete wasn't accustomed to sitting in the passenger seat and started flinching each time Seth came too close to the edge of what looked like a ten-story drop to the river below. Then he flinched and shrieked. It was just a little shriek but coming from someone who always needed to be in control and frowned at any show of emotion, it started Linda and me snickering. The road continued to climb and narrowed even more. The frothing rapids of the Frazer River were suddenly so far below us, they were just a misty strip of white in the distance. Pete's shrieks increased in volume and his flinches almost put him in Seth's lap. By then Linda and I were laughing so hard, we were collapsed in a heap. Seth was desperately driving on the left side of the road to get as far away from the drop-off on the right as possible when we realized a lumber truck was coming the other way. Seth pulled as close to the edge of the gorge as he dared, stopped the car, pulled on the emergency brake and turned on the flashers. The truck ground its way past us. The driver raised a hand to thank Seth for giving him room and continued on his way.

Pete opened his door, gave his final shriek and reared back when he realized Seth's right wheel was so close to the edge of the drop off into the deep gorge there wasn't room for his foot. As soon as Seth was able to pull back into the center of the road, he stopped, turned off the motor and handed Pete the keys. Linda and I were still laughing. Pete was mad at us for days. I didn't care. This was the price he paid for trying to play God. God doesn't shriek. After that, when boredom threatened, Linda or I made a small shriek, looked at each other and started laughing.

Alaska is vast but has few roads. In the ensuing six weeks, we drove every one. We took the car ferry from Valdez to Juneau and waited three days there for the ferry down the coast to Prince Rupert, the first place with a highway across Canada. Like all the trips I had taken with Pete, I had seen some wonderful places. Pete loved to drive. I didn't. I loved to walk. I had just spent two months cooped up in a car. It had been worth it but this campsite was the last place I could walk for the next six days. Pete wanted me to go with him to drive around Juneau. We had done this once. He just wanted to be behind the wheel of the car where he was in control. I wanted to walk the trails around the glacier where we were camped. Seth and Linda had already made it clear the only reason they would ever get in the car again was because it was the only way to get home. This didn't bother Pete but my lack of interest infuriated him. I made what seemed to me a valid argument but he persisted so I said, "No. I'm going to hike the trails here. There's nothing in Juneau I need to see twice." I had been pleasant but all he had heard was no.

"You sure get ugly when you don't get your way," he finally said, as he slammed the car door, gunned the engine and swung into the road with his tires spewing gravel. Mouth open with shock, I watched the car until it was lost in a cloud of dust.

Something basic in my perception of life changed in the two month trip. For the first time since Max had been born, I could see that I might have a future without holding my breath to stave off disaster minute by minute. Without Max's energy-sapping distraction, I faced the fact that Pete wanted a housewife he could keep under his thumb, not an equal partner. Divorce seemed the best answer if I wanted to have a life of my own but I had invested so many years in this marriage, it was hard to walk away.

Working on food accounts as an artist had fostered an interest in nutrition and health. I was appalled at the junk foods touted as healthy and equally dismayed that intelligent people believed everything they saw on TV. I planned to go back to school and study biochemistry as soon as we moved to Pennsylvania. I could see this made Pete uneasy.

I hoped if he saw I could do well in a field other than art, he would eventually see me as a worthwhile, non-threatening individual. I realized this was one last attempt to turn him into Mr Darcy. He told me later that he assumed I would do badly in school and finally settle down and do things his way. We were both wrong.

When I brought home a straight 4.0 average report card at the end of my first semester as a biochemistry major, Pete said, "That's nice," and asked what I had cooked for dinner. When Seth said he had done the same thing and made the high honor roll, Pete sneered and told Seth grades meant absolutely nothing in the *real* world, and then he said, "What difference does it make? You *still* have to get a hall-pass to go to the bathroom."

I praised Seth but he was at an age when my opinion didn't count. All he heard was his father's contempt for what he had done. That was the last time Seth was on the high school honor roll.

Chapter 53

Max loved parachuting and was good at it. But once he got over the thrill of being paid to jump out of airplanes and shoot guns, boredom set in and he and the Army were often at odds. His problem with reading other people and following what he felt were arbitrary rules, coupled with his recurring love of explosives, made his last year and a half in the Army a disaster. He didn't have the smarts to hide his brains and was bullied physically and psychologically by barely literate men who resented him.

He was like a clumsy kid trying to pick his way through an uncharted minefield. Eventually he took one misstep too many.

He had the capacity to work hard but he liked to choose where he spent his energy. The Army began to feel like a strict high school with spit-shined shoes and very short hair. He didn't have a problem with the shoes but decided to let his hair grow. We didn't hear from him for months. I assumed he was still in Germany jumping out of airplanes. I finally got a letter from Max. I recognized his handwriting but was confused to see a postmark from a base in Kansas. There was no return address.

The letter was full of anger, he blamed me for everything that had ever gone wrong in his life and informed me I would never see him again. I should have been delighted at this possibility but the habit of loving this exasperating child overrode any self-preservation.

I was frightened. I knew something terrible had happened. The letter gave no reason why he was in Kansas, nor what had triggered this outpouring of pure vitriol. Months went by without another word from him. He finally called Pete in New York. He needed a lawyer. It turned out he hadn't done anything to harm anyone else. He was still obsessed with guns and explosives, had serious issues with authority figures and pushed all the wrong buttons of the people in control of his life in the army.

Max finally got out of the Army and dragged himself home. The next six months felt like six years. He was an angry wreck and seemed determined to pull the rest of the family into the carnage he had created.

Pete had a studio apartment in New York, furnished with items he chose without any help from me. It was like a jewel. It had the best sound system he had ever owned, a new television, Danish designer furniture, cutlery and china from a high end store, and handsome linens. It was a classic New York bachelor's apartment: the first apartment he ever had all to himself and he was loving it. He saw every movie, every play, became an expert on good restaurants. This was the life he really wanted. He came to Pennsylvania most Fridays to do his laundry but rarely lasted the whole weekend.

I envied him but wasn't smart enough then to realize what a disservice I had done him by marrying him when he gave me the choice.

Max had taken the GED shortly after he enlisted and aced it. As soon as he could after he got home, he took the SAT and had high enough scores to get into the engineering school where my father earned his engineering degree.

Max was comfortable with other engineers. They thought he was normal, which was a delightful first for him. A compulsive worker, he satisfied all the requirements for a Chemical Engineering degree and a Mechanical Engineering degree but balked at taking double doses of the humanities courses required for Bachelor of Science degrees in both disciplines.

Most students took the humanities courses one at a time sprinkled through the four years. Max had managed to avoid them. With his literal mind, he was offended when philosophy and psychology professors stated what he considered pure speculation as scientific facts. He flunked everything but the language requirement.

He spent the summer depressed. On the fourth of July he and Seth were setting off home-made fire-crackers when Max made the mistake that gives fire-crackers a bad name. He didn't realize a fuse was already lit and blew off the tips of his right thumb and first two fingers. This required reconstructive surgery that continued into the beginning of the fall semester.

Pete called the dean; certain Max had lost his chance at a college degree. The dean was unfazed. He said engineers were always blowing parts of themselves off. He suggested Max take a semester of intense language school in Germany since he already spoke some German. If he came back fluent enough to speak it, write it, read and understand engineering journals written in German and wrote a paper on the German government, he would satisfy the humanities requirement for his BSc. It was a great college.

Chapter 54

Max's odd mind-set was finally a saleable asset as an engineer. His ability to think outside the box kept him employed. When he encountered a theoretically unsolvable problem, he instinctively approached it wondering *how* he could solve it, not *if*. And more often than not, he *did* solve it. This made the bureaucratic nay-sayers wild and repeatedly put him in the awkward position of inadvertently showing up the people who had originally proven the problem was insoluble.

Fortunately, he worked for large firms, was willing to go anywhere, at any time and had smart people in charge who recognized the value of a wildly creative mind in a trouble-shooter. Particularly one who knew and followed every Federal regulation when he worked in facilities where pharmaceuticals were manufactured.

Realizing that it would give him an additional edge, he put himself through a master's degree in Electrical Engineering while working full time (often in another country) and sent us all formal invitations to his graduation ceremony. June 15th 1966 was a perfect day. The sky was a clear blue so vivid it looked as improbable as a re-colored Technicolor background. There was a gentle breeze which cleared away the odor of the car exhaust and oil refineries usually a part of West Philadelphia ambience. The streets were washed clean, thanks to a two hour deluge the night before.

Seth collected Linda, Andrea and me and drove us all into Philadelphia. Pete met us there. Max was waiting for us. He glowed. This was *his* turf and he was an assured, gracious host. We talked with him briefly and then made our way to the auditorium.

Even though we were quite a distance from the stage, I had no trouble recognizing Max. The vivid orange lining of the master's degree hood was draped around the neck of his black gown. When he turned to face the university president, he automatically straightened and pulled his shoulders back. I felt sudden tears; it was the same gesture that had identified him in the Florida courtroom. Only now his face was wreathed by a grin of hard-won success. My tears overflowed unchecked. I didn't care who saw them.

Ever since I first heard it as a child, I had been baffled by the biblical fable of the prodigal son. I finally understood the point of the story. We expected the other kids to succeed, we white-knuckled Max all the way through his life breathlessly waiting for the next mind-numbing disaster.

This joy in his success was straight from the gut. I wasn't alone. Pete and the kids felt it too. We had all lived for years with Max's threatening behavior hanging over our heads. When he walked across the stage and got his degree, he glowed with well deserved pride. I gave a profound sigh of relief.

He had battled with missed deadlines at the university because he was out of the country so often but he managed to convince administrators and faculty that he had to stay employed to afford the degree and he had to be willing to go where his company needed him at any moment to stay employed.

His tenacity worked to his advantage for once. He presented cogent, winning arguments and won.

Pete and I grinned through the whole day. I kept thinking of the father in the fable and knew how he felt. I would have been thrilled to give Max all my sheep, gold, land and donkeys. I would have given him my first-born son but I already had.

EPILOGUE

With the help of a smart, pragmatic marriage counselor, degrees from two top-notch universities, a good job and my children's support, I was able to see that my own opinion of me was all that mattered. And I liked what I saw.

Pete and I were separated for a long time and finally divorced. He said we had "a perfect marriage until those women's libbers got hold of me."

The scariest part of this comment was that he believed what he said. The kids just shrugged and said, "Of course. It *was* a perfect marriage for *him* and that was all he saw." A friend asked if I could remember what had been the last straw that finally triggered the divorce. Without a moment's hesitation I said, "It wasn't one straw; it was a haystack."

Andrea is an artist with a special talent for print making. She has battled a chronic illness with fierce determination, courage and informed denial since she was eighteen. A tough little person, she won't let anyone tell her she can't do something because she is ill. Her husband Chris is a positive, loving man who supports her belief she can do anything at all. They have lively five-year-old twins, Ainsley and Aidan, who are natural comedians.

Seth finally decided he wanted to shape his own future and has aced every thing he has tackled ever since. He inherited Pete's quick wit but not the need to put other people down. He is a pilot for a major airline, makes beautiful, much sought after guitars, is married to Vicki, an equally smart and witty woman and has a gem of a daughter Emily, who he appreciates and adores. She has inherited her parents' smart wit and skill at Solitaire.

Max's wife Jacqueline is a gem. Also an engineer, she thinks he is great. He knows how lucky he is and cherishes her. She

249

holds her own at killer Solitaire. Max currently works out of state but they spend most weekends together.

Linda used her managerial skills and understanding of people to become a successful marketing executive in New York City. She now works in Pennsylvania doing much the same thing but in a slightly more relaxed atmosphere. Her recently remodeled house is party central for the whole family. She is a great cook and baker but we would show up if she served store-bought macaroni and cheese. We all like her company. She has two daughters, Caitlin and Courtney, who have talents that continue to amaze us. Like their mother, they are lethal at killer solitaire. Linda is engaged to Jody, a warm funny man who makes her happy and delights the entire family.

The portrait of Linda and Max hangs on a prominent wall in my house. Recently, I asked Max why he put his hand over his mouth every time his father held the camera up to his eye. This time he answered.

"Linda told me to cover my mouth each time Dad was about to take the picture."

"Did she say *why*?"

"She said something bad would get me if I let Dad photograph my mouth."

"She didn't say *what* would happen?"

"No but I knew if Linda said it would be bad, it would be *really* bad."

Now when I look at the picture, I can't help smiling. There's nothing significant in the covered mouth or the worried expression. Max was caught between two explicit orders. His father and his older sister were both in a position to harm him. He was wise to be worried. Any normal kid would have been.

I hated the word *normal* when Pete used it but I love it when I can apply it to Max.

BOOKS

O is a symbol of the world, of oneness and unity. In different cultures it also means the "eye," symbolizing knowledge and insight. We aim to publish books that are accessible, constructive and that challenge accepted opinion, both that of academia and the "moral majority."

Our books are available in all good English language bookstores worldwide. If you don't see the book on the shelves ask the bookstore to order it for you, quoting the ISBN number and title. Alternatively you can order online (all major online retail sites carry our titles) or contact the distributor in the relevant country, listed on the copyright page.

See our website **www.o-books.net** for a full list of over 500 titles, growing by 100 a year.

And tune in to myspiritradio.com for our book review radio show, hosted by June-Elleni Laine, where you can listen to the authors discussing their books.

MySpiritRadio